GLOBALVIEWPOINTS

Arms Sales, Treaties, and Violations

Other Books in the Global Viewpoints Series

GLOBALVIEWPOINTS

Arms Sales, Treaties, and Violations

Rita Santos, Book Editor

GREENHAVEN
PUBLISHING

Published in 2019 by Greenhaven Publishing, LLC
353 3rd Avenue, Suite 255, New York, NY 10010

Cover image: STRINGER/AFP/Getty Images

Cataloging-in-Publication Data

Names: Santos, Rita, editor.
Title: Arms sales, treaties, and violations / edited by Rita Santos.
Description: New York : Greenhaven Publishing, 2019. | Series: Global viewpoints |
  Includes bibliographical references and index. | Audience: Grades 9–12.
Identifiers: LCCN ISBN 9781534503496 (library bound) | ISBN 9781534503502 (pbk.)
Subjects: LCSH: Arms transfers—Juvenile literature. | Illegal arms transfers—Juvenile
  literature. | Defense industries—Juvenile literature.
Classification: LCC HD9743.A2 A767 2019 | DDC 382/.456234—dc23

Manufactured in the United States of America

Website: http://greenhavenpublishing.com

Contents

Chapter 2: The Effects of the Arms Trade

Chapter 3: Nuclear Proliferation

Chapter 4: Strategies for Addressing the Arms Trade

Foreword

> *"The problems of all of humanity can only be solved by all of humanity."*
> —*Swiss author Friedrich Dürrenmatt*

Global interdependence has become an undeniable reality. Mass media and technology have increased worldwide access to information and created a society of global citizens. Understanding and navigating this global community is a challenge, requiring a high degree of information literacy and a new level of learning sophistication.

Building on the success of its flagship series, Opposing Viewpoints, Greenhaven Publishing has created the Global Viewpoints series to examine a broad range of current, often controversial topics of worldwide importance from a variety of international perspectives. Providing students and other readers with the information they need to explore global connections and think critically about worldwide implications, each Global Viewpoints volume offers a panoramic view of a topic of widespread significance.

Drugs, famine, immigration—a broad, international treatment is essential to do justice to social, environmental, health, and political issues such as these. Junior high, high school, and early college students, as well as general readers, can all use Global Viewpoints anthologies to discern the complexities relating to each issue. Readers will be able to examine unique national perspectives while, at the same time, appreciating the interconnectedness that global priorities bring to all nations and cultures.

Material in each volume is selected from a diverse range of sources, including journals, magazines, newspapers, nonfiction books, speeches, government documents, pamphlets, organization newsletters, and position papers. Global Viewpoints is truly global, with material drawn primarily from international sources available in English and secondarily from US sources with extensive international coverage.

Features of each volume in the Global Viewpoints series include:

- An **annotated table of contents** that provides a brief summary of each essay in the volume, including the name of the country or area covered in the essay.

- An **introduction** specific to the volume topic.

- A **world map** to help readers locate the countries or areas covered in the essays.

- For each viewpoint, an **introduction** that contains notes about the author and source of the viewpoint explains why material from the specific country is being presented, summarizes the main points of the viewpoint, and offers three **guided reading questions** to aid in understanding and comprehension.

- **For further discussion questions** that promote critical thinking by asking the reader to compare and contrast aspects of the viewpoints or draw conclusions about perspectives and arguments.

- A worldwide list of **organizations to contact** for readers seeking additional information.

- A **periodical bibliography** for each chapter and a **bibliography of books** on the volume topic to aid in further research.

- A comprehensive **subject index** to offer access to people, places, events, and subjects cited in the text.

Global Viewpoints is designed for a broad spectrum of readers who want to learn more about current events, history, political science, government, international relations, economics, environmental science, world cultures, and sociology—students doing research for class assignments or debates, teachers and faculty seeking to supplement course materials, and others wanting to understand current issues better. By presenting how people in various countries perceive the root causes, current consequences, and proposed solutions to worldwide challenges, Global Viewpoints volumes offer readers opportunities to enhance their global awareness and their knowledge of cultures worldwide.

Introduction

> *"The unleashing of [the] power of the atom has changed everything but our modes of thinking and thus we drift toward unparalleled catastrophes."*
> *Albert Einstein*

The buying and selling of weapons is big business. The United States is the largest supplier and consumer of small and large arms. Its military budget in 2017 was $523.9 billion. While most of that money funds military bases around the globe, a good deal of it is also spent on weapons. In 2015, the US military spent close to $17 billion on missiles and munitions alone.[1]

But the United States isn't the only country where arms deals are big business. All around the world, arms sales both large and small is a multibillion-dollar industry. When well-regulated and used by the proper authorities, weapons can help protect civilians. However, there is a dark side to arms deals as well. After all, it is impossible to have an armed conflict without weapons.

For countries with few exports or natural resources, weapons sales can offer economic independence from wealthier nations. However, most weapons are complicated pieces of equipment that require parts from all over the world. Few nations have the resources and technology to fully produce weapons on their own. So, nations looking for economic dependence quickly find themselves equally dependent on imports. Another complication is knowing who to sell to. Nations and private business are eager to make a profit on weapons sales, but they must also avoid selling to their enemies or to governments who would use them on their own civilians.

While armed conflict remains a destructive fact of life, the United Nations attempts to enact treaties that will preserve lives during times of conflict. Arms treaties like the Arms Trade Treaty (ATT) and the Nuclear Non-Proliferation Treaty (NPT) were designed to help control and regulate the sales of arms worldwide. The main goal of the ATT is to prevent weapons from being sold to governments or groups who have committed human rights violations. Even with tough regulations, the black market for illegally sold weapons will remain. In 2016, just over 18,000 guns were stolen in the United States alone.[2] Civilians are the largest casualty of the illicit small arms trade.

As the threat of large-scale war between nations seems to be declining, the deadliness of weapons has only improved. In Africa, lighter guns have made it easier for terrorist organizations to use children as soldiers.[3] The atomic bomb is so powerful that the mere threat that it might be used is thought to be enough to prevent conflict. Scientists are positive that a nuclear war would result in a "nuclear winter," potentially killing all of humankind. Even Albert Einstein, who helped convince the US government to pursue nuclear weapons, said "Had I known that the Germans would not succeed in producing an atomic bomb, I never would have lifted a finger." Despite the wishes of civilians and the regrets of past geniuses, the arms industry continues to innovate. It is in the arms industry's best interest for armed conflict to continue.

How can nations balance the need for defense while also reigning in the arms industry's need for profits? In diverse viewpoints from around the world, *Global Viewpoints: Arms Sales, Treaties, and Violations* presents a global perspective of how arms sales affect different parts of the globe and how nations are attempting to regulate the problem using arms treaties. Students will learn how governments are coming together to protect citizens and regulate the arms industry.

Endnotes

1. Sky Gould and Jeremy Bender, "Here's How the US Military Spends Its Billions," Business Insider, August 29, 2015. http://www.businessinsider.com/how-the-us-military-spends-its-billions-2015-8

2. "ATF" Releases 2016 Summary of Firearms Reported Lost and Stolen from FFLs," Bureau of Alcohol, Tobacco, Firearms and Explosives," April 11, 2017. https://www.atf.gov/news/pr/atf-releases-2016-summary-firearms-reported-lost-and-stolen-ffls

3. Eben Kaplan, "Child Soldiers Around the World," Council on Foreign Relations, December 2, 2005. https://www.cfr.org/backgrounder/child-soldiers-around-world

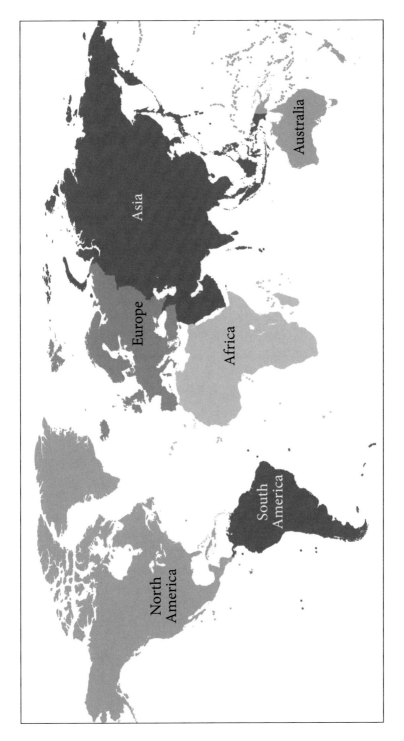

CHAPTER 1

Arms Sales Around the World

In the United States, Arms Deals Are Big Business

Stockholm International Peace Research Institute

In the following viewpoint, the Stockholm International Peace Research Institute (SIPRI) provides an overview of some of the largest arms dealers in the world. While countries like the United States have seen a drop in revenue, arms sales continues to be a multibillion-dollar industry. Lockheed Martin, an American company, remains the largest arms producer in the world. However, countries like South Korea have seen an increase in arms sales in order to meet their military's growing demands. Stockholm International Peace Research Institute is an independent international institute dedicated to research into conflict, armaments, arms control, and disarmament.

As you read, consider the following questions:

1. How does the SIPRI define an arms sale?
2. According to the SIPRI, who are the "emerging producers" of arms sales?
3. How much money did the United States make on arms sales in 2015?

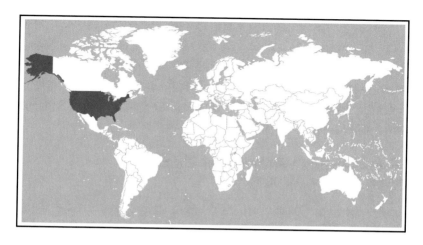

Sales of arms and military services by the largest arms-producing and military services companies—the SIPRI Top 100—totaled $370.7 billion in 2015 according to new data on the international arms industry released today by SIPRI.

The sales of arms and military services companies in the SIPRI Top 100 have fallen for the fifth consecutive year. However, at only a 0.6 per cent decline, the slight decrease may signal a possible reversal of the downward sales trend observed since 2011.

US Companies Still Way Ahead Despite Falling Revenues

Companies based in the United States continue to dominate the Top 100 with total arms sales amounting to $209.7 billion for 2015. Arms sales by US companies in the Top 100 decreased by 2.9 per cent compared with 2014—the fifth consecutive year of decline.

"Lockheed Martin remains the largest arms producer in the world," says Aude Fleurant, Director of SIPRI's Arms and Military Expenditure Programme. "However, US companies' arms sales are constrained by caps on US military spending, delays in deliveries of major weapon systems and the strength of the US dollar, which has negatively affected export sales."

Many of the larger US arms-producing companies divested their military services activities after 2010 due to falling demand. A number of the new, smaller companies created by this process have consolidated and have built up sufficient revenue to rank in the Top 100 for 2015; three such companies are CSRA, Engility and Pacific Architects and Engineers.

West European Arms Sales Up in 2015 After Falls in 2014

Arms sales by companies in Western Europe listed in the SIPRI Top 100 for 2015 rose by 6.6 per cent in real terms compared with 2014, with total combined revenues from arms sales amounting to $95.7 billion. This increase contrasts with the notable drop in West European companies' revenues from arms sales recorded between 2013 and 2014.

The combined arms sales of the six French companies listed in the Top 100 totaled $21.4 billion in 2015, a rise of 13.1 per cent compared with 2014, when most of those companies recorded a fall in arms sales. The increase in French companies' arms sales has acted as an important driver for the recent growth in arms sales in Western Europe.

"Major arms export deals in 2015, such as those to Egypt and Qatar, have increased French arms companies' sales," says Fleurant. "A 67.5 per cent surge in arms sales by Dassault Aviation Group seems to be mainly the result of such exports."

The three German companies listed in the Top 100 continued to increase their combined sales (by 7.4 per cent) in 2015. Companies in the Top 100 based in the United Kingdom reversed the downward trend recorded in 2014 with a 2.8 per cent rise in their combined arms sales in 2015.

Continued Growth in Sales by the Russian Arms Industry

The combined arms sales of the 11 Russian companies in the 2015 Top 100 reached $30.1 billion, representing 8.1 per cent of the total Top 100 arms sales for 2015 and an increase of 6.2 per cent compared with 2014. Ten out of the 11 companies listed have increased their arms sales in 2015.

"Profiting from the Russian military modernization programme, most of the top Russian companies have increased their arms sales in constant roubles," says SIPRI Senior Researcher Siemon Wezeman. "However, all Russian companies in the SIPRI Top 100 for 2015 are ranked lower than they were in 2014 because the pace of the growth in their arms sales has slowed."

South Korea Leading the Rise of Emerging Producers in the Top 100

Emerging producers and other established producers account for 9.5 per cent of the Top 100 arms sales for 2015 with a combined total of $34.5 billion.* This represents an increase of 3.0 per cent for other established producers compared with 2014 and a rise of 15.9 per cent for emerging producers. The significant growth in emerging producers' arms sales is mostly attributable to South Korean companies, which increased sales by 31.7 per cent in 2015.

"All South Korean companies show higher arms sales in 2015, reflecting their growing capacity to meet the South Korean Ministry of Defense's demand and their ongoing success in the international market," says Wezeman. "LIG Nex1 increased its arms sales by 34.7 per cent compared with 2014, and Korea Aerospace Industry's arms sales rose by 51.7 per cent." Poongsan (an ammunition and propellant producer), DSME (a shipbuilder) and Hanwha Thales (a weapon systems producer) were new South Korean entrants to the Top 100 in 2015.

National efforts among the emerging producers to develop their arms industries have shown mixed results in 2015. The combined arms sales of India's ranked companies grew by 9.3 per cent compared with 2014, while the combined sales of Turkish companies rose by 10.2 per cent. Embraer, the sole Brazilian company in the Top 100, recorded a 28.1 per cent decline in its arms sales in 2015.

The SIPRI Arms Industry Database

The SIPRI Arms Industry Database was created in 1989. It contains financial and employment data on arms-producing companies worldwide. Since 1990, SIPRI has published data on the arms sales and employment of the 100 largest of these arms-producing companies in the SIPRI Yearbook.

Arms sales' are defined by SIPRI as sales of military goods and services to military customers, including sales for domestic procurement and sales for export. Changes are calculated in real terms and country comparisons are only for the same companies over different years.

* The "emerging producers" category covers companies located in Brazil, India, South Korea and Turkey. The "other established producers" category covers companies located in Australia, Israel, Japan, Poland, Singapore and Ukraine.

In the Middle East, Arms Sales Offer Political and Economic Benefits to Countries

Joe Stork

In the following viewpoint, Joe Stork argues that the Middle East relies on arms production. Countries often want to increase arms production in order to limit their dependence on foreign nations. However, few countries can do so without the help of imports. The countries of the Middle East are also highly militarized due to the region's geopolitical importance, which makes its high output of arms production worth noting. Stork is deputy director of Human Rights Watch's Middle East and North Africa division.

As you read, consider the following questions:

1. Which country is the largest Third World arms exporter?
2. What political reasons do countries have for boosting arms production?
3. What were the goals of the Arab Organization of Industries (AOI)

Forty years ago, arms production in the Middle East was limited to a few small factories producing rifles and ammunition. Today, arms production has become a very big business in the region, with annual output worth more than $4 billion and rising.

"Arms Industries of the Middle East," by Joe Stork, Middle East Research and Information Project. Reprinted by permission.

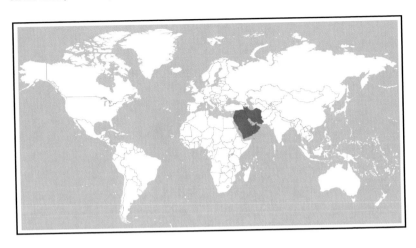

Of the 23 Third World countries with extensive military production, five are in the Middle East. One Middle Eastern state, Israel, is the largest Third World arms exporter and has one of the largest arms industries in the world. Egypt and Turkey are the other two major arms producers in the region, followed by Iran and Pakistan. Munitions and small arms producers include Algeria, Ethiopia, Iraq, Jordan, Morocco, Saudi Arabia, Syria, Sudan and Tunisia.

The Middle East is not the only region of the world where military expenditures have soared and military industries grown considerably. But relative to population, militarization in the Middle East is especially pronounced. The region's geopolitical importance and its oil resources have given rise to wars and threats of wars throughout the period since World War II. Countries establish weapons industries for a variety of reasons. On the political side, regimes seek reduced dependence on outside suppliers, local prestige and regional status. Economically such enterprises may reduce foreign exchange needs, and contribute to the development of an industrial base. In fact, dependence on outside suppliers is only modified: few countries can reduce the import content of their military production below 30 percent.

Turkey, Egypt and Israel need to increase export earnings. Local arms production can replace arms imports and thus save on foreign exchange. Arms companies in the developed countries are ready to shift part of their production overseas to take advantage of cheaper labor costs and to gain access to local markets. Production is often licensed through foreign firms. Weapons systems designed domestically are usually modeled on systems previously imported. The US, Britain, France, West Germany and Soviet Union account for some 85 percent of all licenses. Of these, the US has provided the most, the Soviet Union the least.

Egypt

Egyptian arms production dates back to the period of Muhammad Ali's rule in the 1820s. Comprehensive and of high quality, it included warships, artillery, rifles, bombs and ammunition. Both resources and market were strictly domestic. But under European pressure, facilities were disbanded in the 1840s.

Egypt began modern arms production after World War II with help from German, Swedish and French experts. The government built ammunition and small arms factories in the mid-1950s. An aircraft factory was set up at Helwan, near Cairo, in 1950 to produce primary trainers and prototypes of fighters, and the Helwan Engine Company was set up in 1960 to produce aircraft engines. The Sakr Factory for Developed Industries, set up in 1953 in Heliopolis, another Cairo suburb, was a munitions works which began to develop missiles in the 1960s. All of these efforts were based on imported technology. During the 1960s, Egyptian industry built several hundred aircraft; some were exported. But the Soviets, by then Egypt's main arms supplier, discouraged local arms production. The arms factories ran into financial difficulties and many had closed by the end of the 1960s. Apart from light arms manufacture, Egypt's military industry worked only on repair and maintenance of imported weapons.

Egypt broke its special relations with the Soviets after 1973 and turned to the West. The 1973 October war and the increase in oil prices spurred plans for expanded Egyptian military industries. So did the new economic program of infitah, with its goal of opening of the Egyptian economy to foreign companies and expanding exports. The Sadat regime proposed construction of a military-industrial complex called the Arab Organization of Industries (AOI). AOI was based on the idea that the Saudis and their partners would provide the capital; Washington, London and Paris would provide the technology and capital equipment; Egypt would contribute its four existing arms factories—the aircraft and engine factories in Helwan, the Sakr munitions factory in Heliopolis and the Kader factory (aircraft and armor)—and some 15,000 trained workers. AOI was formally set up in 1975 and some assembly and licensing agreements were reached in 1977-1978, but Saudi Arabia and the other Gulf states cut off funding in 1979 in response to the Egyptian-Israeli-US peace treaty. Egypt assumed total control of the consortium at that point, with credits from the US and France and some money from arms exports. Since 1984, there have been reports of renewed Saudi funding.

AOI annual production was about $100 million in the early 1980s. Most of this output was for Egyptian forces, though Egypt exports to Iraq and some other Arab and African states as well. Military Production Industries (MPI) is a government-run arms complex under the Defense Ministry that is separate from AOI. MPI has 15 factories, mainly in Cairo's suburbs. Its $240 million annual output of small arms and ammunition is mostly for local use. Together the two consortia oversee 24 factories and have a labor force of between 70,000 and 100,000.

AOI projects have built up the Egyptian aerospace industry. Between 1982 and 1985, the Helwan plant assembled some 37 French Alpha jets with almost half local components including flaps, rudders, tailcones and some avionics. Helwan is now assembling Chinese F-7 (MiG-21) fighters, and is beginning to assemble Mirage 2000 fighters. The Kader factory, perhaps with Saudi financing, is producing 110 Brazilian EMB-312 Tucano trainers, 80 of them for Iraq. The new privately financed Arab-British Helicopter Company is assembling two or three Gazelle light helicopters per month, and Aerospatiale has also agreed to provide technology for assembly of the Super Puma helicopter. Three factories at Helwan assemble, repair and overhaul aircraft engines. Benha Electronics Factory, in a co-production arrangement with Westinghouse, is assembling radar systems. It has a work force of 3,000 and annual turnover of 70 million Egyptian pounds. Egypt designed and developed the Walid armored personnel carrier in the 1960s. A new version, the Fahd, came off the assembly lines in 1984 and several Arab states have placed orders. General Dynamics, the US firm, won a contract in 1984 to build a tank factory outside Cairo. US and British firms have competed for contracts supplying tools for upgrading Soviet artillery. In 1982, Egypt sold Iraq $1 billion worth of refurbished Soviet military hardware, and the arms trade to Iraq has remained brisk.

Egypt currently assembles the British Swingfire anti-tank missile, and versions of the Soviet SA-7 and SA-2 portable surface-to-air missiles, as well as several kinds of air-to-air and air-to-ground missiles. These missiles are mostly built at the Sakr works. Egyptian factories are also turning out increasing quantities of guns and ammunition, some for export. And they are producing military electronics such as radios and telecommunications. France is Egypt's major partner in developing more sophisticated assembly and production facilities. According to one French executive, "Egypt has become a profitable relay between France and the other countries in the region." At a time of declining foreign exchange revenues, Egypt is counting on increasing its arms exports. Since Iraq takes two thirds of Egypt's military exports, an end to the Gulf War could affect Cairo's export plans significantly. Egypt also needs to increase arms exports to make its military industries cost-effective. Gamal al-Sayyid Ibrahim, minister of state for military production, discussing which main battle tank Egypt might assemble, remarked that the choice would not only have to meet Egyptian army requirements but would also have "to satisfy the market around us." Apart from Iraq, some of Egypt's main clients have been Somalia, Oman, Sudan and North Yemen. Shipments to these countries, including Chinese jet fighters and Soviet and US tanks, have been financed by Saudi Arabia and Kuwait. Other important customers have been the Afghan mujahidin and the Washington-backed forces of Hissene Habre in Chad.

Iran

Iran is a textbook case of a country whose small industrial base and determination to acquire state-of-the-art weaponry combined to ensure that it would remain overwhelmingly dependent on foreign manufacturers. With the exception of some aircraft assembly begun in the 1930s and terminated with the outbreak of World War II, Iran has imported most of its weapons from the United States.

Iranian production of small arms and explosives dates back to the 1920s. An ammunition factory at Parchin, in the north of the country, has operated continuously for more than 50 years. By the late 1970s the Royal Armaments Factories in Tehran were manufacturing a wide variety of small arms, including basic infantry rifles and machine guns. Today the production of these and other plants supply Iranian forces in the war with Iraq.

When the Shah decided to expand Iran's military might, he emphasized the air force. In 1969, the parliament obliged by decreeing that a portion of the country's oil revenues be put in a fund for arms imports. In 1970 the Shah established Iran Aircraft Industries (IACI) as a joint venture with Northrop. A repair facility for US-made missiles also was set up at Shiraz.

Between 1970 and 1974, the military's share in total capital expenditures in the country rose from 25 percent to 41 percent of the total, and many different industrial sectors—automotive, chemical, mechanical—had some military dimension to them. A huge military-industrial complex was begun near Isfahan, and by 1978 spare parts for tanks and helicopters were being manufactured there. The Military Industries Organization was the single largest importer of machine tools in the mid-1970s.

Iran's sizable automobile assembly industry had a military component. Three foreign auto licensers, Jeep (US), British Leyland (maker of the Land Rover) and Daimler-Benz (West Germany) manufactured military vehicles. While tank maintenance and repairs remained a completely military project, the private sector took on the production and repair of military vehicles. In small arms production, French, German and Swedish companies licensed factories owned by Iranian entrepreneurs.

The purchase agreements made by the Shah's government for advanced weapons systems usually included provision of repair facilities and training programs for Iranian technicians. Most of these operations involved replacing rather than repairing defective parts. The IACI experience illustrates the limits of these measures. In 1975, the Iranian government bought out Northrop, and then contracted with Lockheed and General Electric for similar services. By 1977, IACI had a work force of 2,600 in five Iranian cities. Three quarters of these were Iranians, but they were concentrated in management and unskilled jobs. At the core of IACI were some 600 skilled workers from Pakistan, South Korea and the Philippines and 50 technicians from the US.

Other repair and assembly contracts were extensions of sales contracts, giving multinational arms companies easy access to the Iranian market through these local subsidiaries. The Iranian state firms producing and repairing weapons were grouped under the Military Industries Organization and, one step removed, the War Ministry. Many of the same middlemen close to the Peacock Throne who profited handsomely on contracts for importing weapons also had financial interests in these enterprises.

At the time of the revolution in 1979, several of these different arms projects were incomplete. One was the Bell Helicopter joint venture in Isfahan to train 1,500 pilots and 5,000 mechanics and then to assemble a military transport helicopter. This was canceled. The Islamic Republic has continued arms production at a reduced level, but the war with Iraq has been fought largely with imported weapons and ammunition. And the regime has no doubt extended and expanded the local maintenance and repair capacity begun under the Shah.

Israel

Israel's arms industry is the largest and most sophisticated outside the industrialized countries. It predates the state itself, with roots in the small arms and ammunition workshops that grew up in the 1930s and 1940s and eventually became Israeli Military Industries (IMI). Israeli Aircraft Industries (IAI) had its beginnings in the early 1950s.

Israeli arms manufacturing really took off after the 1967 war. The French arms embargo, combined with expanding political and economic clout of the Israeli military and US cooperation, helped make Israel's military-industrial establishment what it is today. There are close links between Israeli arms firms, the scientific and technical elite and the officer corps. As in the US, there is a "revolving door" through which former officers pass from staff positions in the armed forces to executive roles in the arms companies. Military expenditures currently run about $5 billion, approximately a third of Israel's gross domestic product (with approximately the same amount again going to repay foreign debts, most of them military). Over $1 billion of this each year is spent on locally produced arms, of which about 25 percent reflects the cost of imported parts and licenses.

The US allows its foreign military assistance to be used for Israeli research and development and production of advanced weapons systems, such as the Merkava main battle tank and the Lavi advanced fighter-bomber. Arms manufacturing has become an important part of Israel's industrial sector, and employs some 60,000, more than one fifth of the industrial work force in the country. IAI (20,000 employees), IMI (15,000) and Tadiran (10,000) are Israel's three largest industrial firms. Metal products, machinery and electronics sectors (of which military production is an important part) were the fastest growing industrial sectors in the country in the 1970s—12 percent a year as against eight percent overall. Military sales abroad of around $1 billion per year are critical to the country's balance of payments. Military production includes a large value-added component and is thus highly profitable. For some firms, such as Iscar Blades, some 90 percent of their market (including civilian goods) is overseas; for many, exports account for more than half their output.

The development of Israel's military industries moved from repair and maintenance to licensed production and finally local design and manufacture. Israel's close ties with advanced arms manufacturing countries, first France and then the United States, was key. Israeli engineers, for instance, were apparently involved in the original Mirage design work in France. In any case, their familiarity with the production process enabled IAI to procure or manufacture the necessary forgings and preformed parts. Israel's first locally produced warplane, the Kfir, had a Mirage-based airframe and the engine of an F-4 Phantom.

Maintenance and servicing is now part of Israeli military exports. IAI currently has a contract to service and upgrade US military helicopters in Europe, and many countries which import US or French weapons systems go to Israel for service contracts. Finally, Israel reconditions and re-exports surplus or outmoded IDF equipment from the US and France, and captured Soviet weapons.

Israel has developed a great ability to upgrade and retool imported weapons systems with the addition of locally produced components. This "mix and match" capability is the most significant feature of the Israeli arms industry today. There is no question that US technology is a key feature of Israel's military might. It is difficult to imagine Israeli military industries as they are today without it. But Israel, because of its high state of military readiness and frequent use of weapons systems, has developed a relatively unique capacity to absorb available technology, build on it and produce modifications and even new systems—such as remotely piloted vehicles, which are not produced anywhere else. At the head of Israeli military industries are the large government firms—IAI, IMI, Rafael, the Main Ordnance factory—which are usually the prime contractors. At a second level is an important group of joint ventures with foreign firms which provide technology and capital and in turn profit from Israel's relatively low-cost scientific and engineering work force. General Telephone and Electronics, Control Data and Motorola are long-standing examples. Finally there are perhaps 150 small and highly specialized Israeli firms which subcontract on weapons projects.

Pakistan

Pakistan is the one other country in the Middle East besides Israel approaching nuclear weapons capability. Yet its production of conventional arms remains limited to infantry weapons, ammunition, small ships and one type of aircraft (on license from Saab). Over the last 10 years, the country has also constructed repair and maintenance facilities for French Mirage fighters and Chinese F-6s and tanks.

It seems paradoxical that a country like Pakistan may soon be able to produce a nuclear bomb, yet cannot produce conventional combat aircraft and missiles. Modern aircraft construction requires a developed industrial base and a market sufficiently large to keep unit costs low. It also requires a range and a concentration of skilled scientists. Pakistan's nuclear program is the brainchild of less than a dozen scientists. Its end product, a small number of nuclear bombs, will not become obsolete in a few years or need the continuous high-tech upgrading required by combat aircraft, missiles and other modern armaments.

The arms production facilities constructed under British rule were in the territory that became India after independence. In the 1950s, Pakistan constructed the Pakistan Ordnance Factory. Pakistani military production increased after the 1965 war with India. Today the POF includes 14 separate factories in and around the city of Wah. This is a company town of 225,000 near Islamabad. Wah's lord mayor is Gen. Talat Massoud, current chairman of the POF. The Wah complex manufactures a wide range of munitions and infantry weapons—mortars, recoilless rifles and anti-tank missiles. The POF employs between 30,000 and 50,000 and has an annual production capacity of more than $400 million. It is the country's largest industrial enterprise.

The technology POF uses comes from various suppliers—West German, British, Swiss, American. Pakistan has access to Chinese technology, and through this the Soviet technology incorporated in Chinese weapons. POF-designed 100mm tank rounds are now competing on the world market for customers among the many Third World countries with Soviet and Chinese designed tanks. Some 15 percent of POF's production is for export, which earns more than $30 million in foreign exchange.

In addition, there is the Pakistan Aeronautical Complex employing some 3,500 Pakistanis and a team of Chinese supervisors. Both the Ordnance Factory and the Aeronautical Complex are directly under the Ministry of Defense. The Communication and Electronic industry at Haipur assembles communications equipment for the military.

Pakistan's largest military export is not its weapons but its soldiers. The country is probably the largest exporter of military personnel in the Third World. It supplies commanders, pilots and technicians to many Arab countries, especially in the Gulf, and to other countries as well. Pakistan has also offered its Mirage repair and maintenance facilities to other countries in the region, and invited these countries to invest in joint arms ventures. China's growing military ties with the West are influencing Pakistan's arms industry. China has been Pakistan's backer against Soviet-backed India in the competition for influence in the subcontinent. The Chinese are building a plant in Pakistan to assemble their F-7 fighter. Both governments have approached the US for technology for this project. Chinese airframes will be fitted with US-built engines, avionics and weaponry.

The United States and Russia Participate in the Most Major Arms Transfers

Kate Blanchfield, Pieter D. Wezeman, and Siemon T. Wezeman

In the following viewpoint, Kate Blanchfield, Pieter D. Wezeman and Siemon T. Wezeman uncover trends in global sales of major weapons using data from the Stockholm International Peace Research Institute, which has kept track of arms transfers since the 1950s. As relationships between nations change, so to does the transfer of major weapons systems. While no region of the globe is free of arms deals, their frequency and size does vary. UN trade embargos have successfully limited major weapons transfers to nations like Iran. The authors are researchers from the Stockholm International Peace Research Institute.

As you read, consider the following questions:

1. Which regions account for the most arms imports?
2. What keeps Iran's arms imports relatively low?
3. Which two nations export the most major weapons?

This week, SIPRI released new data on international arms transfers of major weapons. We've picked out some key trends in the data and present the state of arms transfers. All figures come

"The state of major arms transfers in 8 graphics," by Kate Blanchfield, Pieter D. Wezeman, and Siemon T. Wezeman, Stockholm International Peace Research Institute (SIPRI), February 22, 2017. Reprinted by permission.

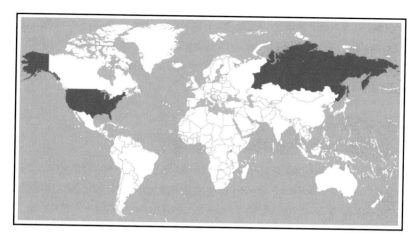

from the SIPRI Arms Transfers Database, which contains data on arms transfers since 1950.

The Volume of International Arms Transfers in the Past 5 Years Was the Highest Since 1990

SIPRI's newly released data shows that the volume of major weapons transfers during 2012–16 increased by 8.4% compared to 2007–11. This is the highest volume of arms transfers during any five-year period since 1990.

SIPRI uses the unique trend-indicator value (TIV) to measure the volume of international transfers of major weapons. This takes into account any transfers of major arms, regardless of the price paid or agreed between the supplier and the recipient.

Asia & Oceania and the Middle East Dominate Arms Imports

SIPRI researchers identified 155 countries that imported major weapons in 2012–16. Nine out of ten of the largest importer countries are in Asia & Oceania and the Middle East, regions that accounted for 43% and 29% of all arms imports, respectively.

India remained the world's biggest arms importer over the past five years, and increased its share of global arms imports from 9.7%

in 2007–11 to 12.8% in 2012–16. Saudi Arabia moved from being the world's eleventh largest arms importer in 2007–11 with 2.9% of the global share to the world's second largest arms importer with an 8.2% share.

The USA Has Shifted Its Arms Exports from Pakistan to India

China, India and Pakistan have been major arms importers over the past 20 years. Pakistan's arms procurement is driven by a perception of India as a threat, while India is concerned about China and Pakistan. Despite these regional tensions, several arms exporters are willing to supply arms to both sides.

China has reduced arms imports, falling from being the world's largest importer in the 2000's to fourth largest in 2016, as its domestic arms industry has become more capable of producing advanced weapons. It is still reliant on imports for certain items, however, such as engines and transport aircraft. India's arms imports have steadily grown over the past 20 years as, unlike China, it has not established a domestic arms industry that can cater to the demands of the Indian military. Pakistan's arms imports have fluctuated over the past 20 years but remain lower than India's.

Russia has been the main arms supplier to both China and India. However, as it does not want to jeopardize its arms trade relation with India, has restricted its arms exports to Pakistan. Between 1997 and 2011, the USA was a major supplier to Pakistan and supplied very few arms to India, but has recently shifted its position and in 2012–16 increased arms exports to India for economic and strategic reasons and significantly reduced exports to Pakistan. China has since become Pakistan's main supplier.

France has been a significant arms supplier to China and Pakistan. Recently, India has made several major orders for French weapons and, with deliveries expected in the coming years, France is set to become a major supplier to India.

Some Large Increases in Arms Imports by States in the South China Sea

The South China Sea has been the subject of increasingly bold rhetoric from the Chinese and US Governments in recent months. Territorial disputes involve various states but have been particularly heated between China, the Philippines and Vietnam. SIPRI data shows that both the Philippines and Vietnam have made large increases in arms imports, particularly of sea-based arms. The Philippines has increased arms imports by 426% between 2012–16 compared to 2007–11 and Vietnam has increased arms imports by 202% over the same period.

Taiwan increased its arms imports by 647% and Indonesia increased arms imports by 70%. Singapore's imports of major weapons decreased by 47%, but it is still absorbing major acquisitions from 2007–11. Malaysia's arms imports dropped after major arms procurement programmes were finished in 2007–11.

Imports by the Arab States of the Gulf Are Much Higher than Imports by Iran

SIPRI data shows that major arms imports by the Arab States of the Gulf and major arms imports to Iran are highly unbalanced. A perceived threat from Iran is a key justification for rising arms imports to several of these states both by the states themselves and the countries exporting to them, such as the USA, UK, France and Germany.

All Arab States of the Gulf except Bahrain increased their major arms imports between 2007–11 and 2012–16. Of the states with tense relations with Iran, Qatar has increased arms imports by 245%, Saudi Arabia by 212%, Kuwait by 175%, and UAE by 63%. Bahrain decreased its arms imports by 19%. Iranian arms imports decreased by 27%.

Iran is currently under a partial UN embargo for arms imports, keeping its imports low. In 2016 Iran received four air defence systems from Russia that are not covered by the embargo, which was the first major arms import by the country since 2007. The USA is the main supplier to the Arab States of the Gulf, supplying over 50% of imports by each of these states except Oman.

The USA and Russia Export over Half of the World's Major Weapons

The USA continued to dominate major arms exports, accounting for 33% of all major arms exports and supplying arms to 103 recipients in 2012–16. Russia was the world's second largest exporter, accounting for 23% of all major arms exports. It supplied arms to 51 recipients in 2012–16 with 70% of its exports going to four countries: India, Vietnam, China and Algeria.

China was the world's third largest exporter of major weapons in 2012–16, having just overtaken Germany, France and the UK, all countries with higher exports during 2007–11. Chinese exports went up by 74% in 2012–16 compared to 2007–11, while French and German exports decreased by 5% and 36%, respectively, and British exports increased by 27%.

In Israel, Conflict with Palestine Benefits International Arms Deals

Taya Govreen-Segal

The following viewpoint is a speech delivered by Taya Govreen-Segal at the "Britain and Palestine: Past History and Future Role" conference, held at Sarum College, Salisbury, UK. The author argues that the arms industry benefits from prolonging and escalating military conflict. She also discusses the effect an arms embargo would have on Israel. Govreen-Segal is an activist and conscientious objector from Israel.

As you read, consider the following questions:

1. What does "battle proven" mean?
2. Why did Israel start importing weapons after the "Yom Kippur" War?
3. Should nations that oppose military conflict participate in arms deals?

I am going to assume that you already know about the violation of human rights in the West Bank and Gaza, that you've heard about the occupation, the military rule and siedge, and focus on one of the forces profiting from this situation and maintaining it: the arms trade.

I would like to start with Gaza 2014. By the end of the 50 days of Operation Protective Edge, Gaza was destroyed. In Gaza, approximately

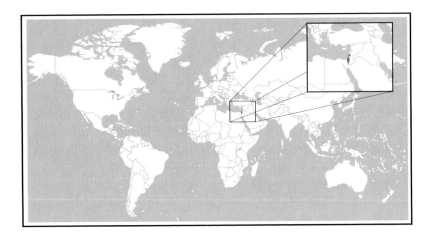

2,200 people were killed, 40–70% of them civilians, while in Israel 5 Israeli civilians, 1 Thai worker, and 66 soldiers were killed.

During the battle in Gaza, newspapers started reporting on new weapons that were put into use. These weapons immediately started being marketed as "battle proven."

As Barbara Opal-Rome wrote in *Defence News* "as it is we do aggressive marketing abroad, but the work of the IDF [Israeli Defence Force] definitely affects the marketing. For the military industries, this operation (Protective Edge) is like drinking a super strong energy drink; it just gives a strong push forward."

How this process happens is explained by General Yoav Galant, commander of operation "Cast Led" in Yotam Feldman's film, "The Lab": Making blood into money. This is how Israel got to be the largest arms exporter in the world, in relation to the size of the economy.

When I'm talking about Israeli military exports, I'm talking about weapons, ammunition and combat aircraft as well as guerrilla warfare training, police training, tactics and tools for riot control, executions, and surveillance and intelligence technologies. This is our contribution to humanity.

In order to understand the arms trade, I find it important to understand how the Israeli arms trade developed, how it receives public backing, and its tight connection to the IDF and the occupation.

The Development of the Arms Trade

Manufacturing arms started as early as the 1920s in illegal workshops hidden from the British Mandate when Zionists who "made aliya"—that is, migrated to historical Palestine, often illegally—discovered that the Arab population already living there didn't think much of their plan of creating a Jewish state in the area.

By 1933, IMI (Israeli Military Industries) was founded, and is one of the largest Israeli arms companies to this day.

Israel was founded in 1948 with the Zionist narrative of a small country surrounded by enemies, of the Jews after the holocaust having nowhere else to go, and of a young country surviving against all odds, thanks to the heroic young people fighting for their homeland. The young state was diplomatically isolated due to the Arab League boycott that threatened to cut trade connections with any country that traded or had diplomatic connections with Israel.

Ben Gurion, the first prime minister of Israel came up with a plan to create trade and diplomatic connections and gain support in the UN: to "start from the periphery" and make connections with nations seeking independence from colonialism, mainly in Africa. One of the main needs of these countries was arms, which Israel was happy to sell to them from its own excess.

A good example is Burma (now Myanmar). In 1954, Burma was the first country to buy arms from Israel, and a year later, the president of Burma was the first president to come on an official visit to Israel.

While Israel created rifles and grenades, it was never self-sufficient in making all of its own weapons, and in these years was very much dependent on France for weapons, including tanks and planes, which it improved and refurbished.

In 1967, following the Six-Day War that France condemned, France stopped arming Israel.

In 1973, in the "Yom Kippur" War, Israel ran out of both weapons and foreign currency. This led Israel to a decision to start exporting arms as a way of securing both needs.

At this point, Europe, the US and the communist bloc were already controlling the arms industry. What could Israel bring to the table? What would be its expertise? The answer was weapons not for fighting an army, but for oppressing and fighting civil uprisings, and controlling the civilian population: a field in which Israel had no lack of experience.

By the early 1980s, arms export was 25% of Israel's export.

In the 90s, the global arms trade underwent two significant changes: following the cold war, there was less of a need for weapons, and Europe and the US changed their values and started considering human rights. This was a good opportunity for Israel to replace them in arming countries that violate human rights.

By Israeli law, Israel is bound by the decisions of the UN Security Council, but this didn't stop Israel from selling weapons to Rwanda during the genocide, former Yugoslavia during the war in Serbia, or South Africa during apartheid.

Even this September, Israeli arms found their way to Myanmar, a country that has been under EU and US embargoes since early 90s.

Israel has the largest security industry in relation to the economy of any country in the world, exporting weapons to 130 different countries. Israel refuses to join the 82 states that have ratified the Arms Trade Treaty and commit to not selling weapons that will be used for genocide, crimes against humanity and violation of human rights, since it fears signing it will lead states to stop trading with Israel.

But Israel isn't only one of the largest exporters of arms, in 2014 it was the 6th largest importer of arms, importing mainly from the US, which provides Israel with a couple billion shekels of military aid every year, of which 75% must be used to buy from the US. From Britain, Israel imports mainly components for combat aircraft and drones, as well as anti-armour ammunition and weapon night sights.

Two examples of arms companies that have UK sites and arm Israel are:

- Elbit Systems: an Israeli company that manufactures the Hermes 900, that was first used in operation "Protective Edge," has 4 sites in the UK
- G4S: a private British security company that provides services for businesses in the West Bank settlements, detention centers, prisons imprisoning Palestinian political prisoners and checkpoints.

Overall, in 2014 Britain granted nearly £12 million worth of export licenses to Israel, and over £25 million worth of export licenses for dual use.

Just an example for what dual use may mean, because it's a very ambiguous term.

On my first visit to an unmanned arms exhibition, I was surprised by the way drones were marketed. Suddenly the main use for drones was "carrying cameras" and "delivering packages." When I asked an IAI (Israel Aerospace industries) representative about a 30 meter long drone whether it could also be used to carry bombs, he answered: "things like using drones for executions in Gaza—we don't talk about them." It's hard for me to imagine that specific one would be considered a dual use item, but maybe the components were? I have no way of knowing.

Public Backing

Moving on to understanding the root of public backing for the arms trade, it's interesting to look at the popular narrative on Israel's security situation; a small country surrounded by enemies, diplomatically isolated because of BDS (Boycott, Divestment and Sanctions), the Jews having nowhere else to go, and of survival against all odds, thanks to our strong army and cutting edge technology.

This narrative—that has stayed almost the same since the founding of the state—is maintained through the educational system and media, and breeds fear. Fear legitimizes military solutions and militarization of society as necessities, as the only way for us to be secure. For example: This picture is of an armed soldier speaking in a school shows a common scenario, and one which I experienced many time throughout high school; soldiers coming into school to share their experience, explain about the different positions in the military, and encourage "meaningful service."

Fear and militarization contribute to a lack of transparency. Anything that has to do with "security" is left to the decision of a small inner circle, far away from public discourse for "security reasons." This is true of anything that has to do with "security," whether it's the question of Israel's possession of nuclear weapons and other weapons of mass destruction, or the security budget. Only 20% of the security budget is transparent in the Knesset (the Israeli Parliament) and Ministry of Finance that need to approve it. Additionally, huge sums of money are added to the initial budget throughout the year without being brought to parliament.

Looking at the defense budget for 2015, after an addition for the month of December, an addition for Operation Protective Edge, a special security addition and the US military aid, the budget is nearly 20% larger than it was initially.

This lack of transparency is also true of the arms trade. The export control department was founded only in 2007 following American pressure, and is part of the ministry of defense. It consists of 2–3 workers, who are responsible for monitoring 8,000 people and companies and 400,000 marketing and export licenses a year. This information on the amount of licenses, along with the figure of 130 countries were only exposed thanks to a freedom of information petition filed by Eitay Mack, an Israeli human rights lawyer, but we have still to discover who are the 8,000 people and companies, since at the moment only 0.02% of their names are exposed.

Arms Trade and the Occupation

This whole industry is dependent on the occupation and the IDF using the arms developed in war and in maintaining the occupation; not only do the Ministry of Defense and the government not stop

The Merchants of Death

Black market trafficking usually takes place on a regional or local level; publicly available data suggests that the multi-ton, inter-continental shipments organized by the 'merchants of death' account for only a small fraction of illicit transfers. Among the most important forms of illicit trafficking is the 'ant trade'—numerous shipments of small numbers of weapons that, over time, result in the accumulation of large numbers of illicit weapons by unauthorized end users. Data analyzed in the Small Arms Survey 2013 indicates that thousands of firearms seized in Mexico are traced to the United States annually. These weapons are often purchased from gun shops in small numbers and then smuggled over the border. While individual transactions occur on a small scale, the sum total of the weapons trafficked into Mexico is large.

While most arms trafficking appears to be conducted by private entities, certain governments also contribute to the illicit trade by deliberately arming proxy groups involved in insurgencies against rival governments, terrorists with similar ideological agendas, or other non-state armed groups. These types of transfers, which are prevalent in Africa and other regions where armed conflict is common, are often conducted in contravention of UN arms embargoes and have the potential to destabilize neighboring countries. In recent years, governments have covertly delivered tens of thousands of small arms and light weapons to various armed groups in Somalia despite a long-standing UN arms embargo. As revealed in the Small Arms Survey 2012, these weapons range from Kalashnikov-pattern assault rifles to third-generation SA-18 MANPADS, one of which was used to shoot down a Belarusian cargo aircraft delivering supplies intended for peacekeepers in March 2007.

The prices of illicit firearms and their relation to security dynamics have attracted interest among journalists and researchers for some time. In the Small Arms Survey 2013 finds a clear link between illicit market prices in Lebanon and reported fatalities during the first 19 months of the conflict in Syria. The particularly strong correlation between ammunition prices in Lebanon and fatalities in Syria underlines the value of monitoring ammunition prices. Yet available reporting from conflict zones has tended to neglect this important piece of the puzzle, focusing on prices for the most common weapons instead.

"Illicit Trafficking," Small Arms Survey.

the exports, they back it and assist them. Only recently it was revealed that the Ministry of Defense gives arms dealers letters of recommendation in which it states that the given weapon was successfully used by IDF soldiers.

This is also visible in the ISDEF, Israel's largest arms exhibit, that is advertised as the best place to "meet your counterparts from Israel such as end users and decision makers from the: IDF, MOD (Ministry of Defense), Police, Prison Service, Fire Department, SAR (search and rescue), Defense Industries, Civil Security Agencies, and Government offices." It also states that there will be "international officials and industry professionals from over 90 countries" but it is impossible to find a list of the countries.

Attending this exhibit as a journalist, it was the first time I was exposed to the arms trade, and I was shocked by how normal it seemed, all these people walking around looking at weapons that are "battle proven," tested and proven to kill people, yet the whole atmosphere was just like any other exhibit, they could have been selling cameras or cosmetics just the same.

But who are these arms dealers? Many of them are former high-ranking officers, some still in reserve, going back and forth between the military and the industry. The IDF needs these the military industries to develop systems for it, while arms companies need the reputation of the IDF to promote overseas sales.

This Revolving door happens on a few levels:

- ex-combatants from special units go to be security guards in Saudi Arabia or Kenya (How would the recruiters in these countries even get the names of the ex-combatants?)

- Civil Administration Graduates go into consulting services, based on their experience in controlling civil population under military rule in the West Bank, and doing things like issuing entry permits to Palestinians.

- High ranking officers and generals go into export and mediation. Mediation is assisting other countries in selling to each other. In most places this kind of work requires a permit, but not in Israel.

This means that the generals, who choose to go to war, are invested in the new weapons used in combat as an advertisement for the products of their associates - products that can later be sold as "battle proven."

Like some of the historical uses of the arms trade, also nowadays the arms trade is used as a diplomatic tool: for example, selling arms to Rwanda and Nigeria in return for them abstaining in the UN Security Council vote on recognition of Palestine.

Another example is arms given at a discount to Rwanda and Uganda in return for them accepting asylum seekers from Sudan and Eritrea.

And if you still aren't convinced, I would like to let the arms dealers speak for themselves, one said to "Haarez": "A scenario in which there won't be a large military operation in 20 years will severely hurt the arms industries."

The question remaining is how we work against it. In Hamushim, we focus on Israeli society: by spreading information and campaigning we try and change the narrative of the military industries as necessary for security and shift the discourse to their part in waging war and profiting from it.

General Yoav Galant spoke about the hypocrisy of countries condemning war and buying the arms tested in it, and I tend to agree. Anyone who wants this bloody conflict to end has to stop fueling it with arms. And this is true for any conflict.

Here in Europe, it looks like things are moving in the right direction: Israeli arms companies have been requested by the IDF to develop parts that up till now have been purchased from Europe because the supply isn't steady enough to rely on, and they fear that items may be banned from export to Israel.

While it may seem that an arms embargo would have no effect on Israel, since it would be able to make its own weapons, this is not completely true. In addition to Israel being the 6th largest military importer, the agreements Israel have with the US stop it from manufacturing products that compete with those of American companies. Also, 75% of Israeli security manufacturing is for export. The Israeli military industries currently focus on developing innovative and new weapons or additions to existing weapons that may be used as a surprise in battlefield and will give a strategic advantage. Will it be financially feasible to develop arms knowing they can only be used by the IDF and not later be sold as battle proven?

Looking at the British law, Britain has every reason to stop arms trade with Israel. According to British law, arms should not be sold if there is a risk that they will be used for internal repression, aggravate existing tensions or conflicts, and should take into account the buyer country's respect for international law. So according to its own laws Britain has every reason to stop trading arms with Israel.

I would like to finish with an action that I find inspiring. This Elbit rooftop occupation stopped manufacturing for two days during Operation Protective Edge, and the charges against the activists were dropped because Elbit didn't want to expose what it was manufacturing fearing that may prove its activity was unlawful.

As activists interested in promoting a just peace between the Jordan river and the Mediterranean sea, stopping arms trade with Israel should be high up on our list of priorities. Arms trade with Israel is one of the most direct ways other countries are involved in the occupation and they should be pressured to stop that involvement. The Elbit rooftop occupation is just one of many ways to target this involvement.

In Africa, Illegal Small Arms Trade Fuels Conflict

United Nations

In the following viewpoint, the United Nations presents findings that the small arms trade contributed to violence and destabilization in many regions of Africa. The UN often holds conferences where nations can discuss international issues. In June 2006, the UN held a conference to explore how the illegal sale of small arms, like guns, was impacting conflict in African nations. The United Nations is dedicated to creating a better world by facilitating peaceful communication between nations.

As you read, consider the following questions:

1. What is the Programme of Action?
2. Why did speakers from the African continent call for a global crackdown in illegal arms deals?
3. In Liberia, what was one of the major fallouts of the illicit sale of small arms?

The United Nations conference targeting the $1 billion-a-year illicit trade in small arms continued today with speakers from the African continent among those calling urgently for a global crack down on illegal arms dealers and tighter arms regulations—especially the activities of brokers—whose deadly wares often fell

From "Illicit Small Arms Trade in Africa Fuels Conflict, Contributes to Poverty, Stalls Development, Says Speakers on Second Day of UN Review Conference," United Nations, June 27, 2006. Reprinted with the permission of the United Nations.

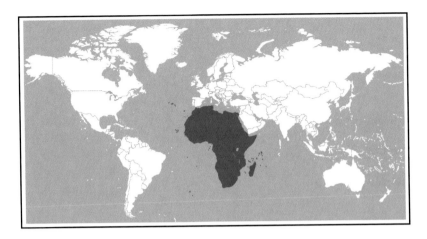

into the hands of non-State actors and fueled conflict, contributed to poverty, and stalled development in their fragile countries.

On day two of the General Assembly's review of worldwide efforts to implement the Programme of Action of its 2001 special session on preventing, combating and eradicating the illicit trade in small arms and light weapons in all its aspects, diplomats from developing countries—some emerging from conflict and others coping with the fallout from bloody civil strife—called for transparency and accountability in small arms production and transfers, weapons registries, and an international code of conduct to help them stem the massive flows of small arms circulating throughout their countries and moving unchecked across porous borders.

Many would agree that Liberia was one of the countries best placed to testify to the devastating breadth of the small arms scourge, said Conmay Wesseh, Deputy Minister for International Cooperation and Economic Integration in the long-troubled West African country's Foreign Affairs Ministry. He painted a vivid picture of his homeland's brutal 14-year civil war, which had been fueled by illegal guns and light artillery. One of the more tragic consequences had been that youth had borne the brunt of the armed violence, and they were still suffering—struggling to cope with high HIV/AIDS rates, low levels of education and poor employment.

Despite the unprecedented impediments, Liberia had committed itself to tackling the proliferation of, and traffic in, small arms. The new Government—the first on the African continent to be headed by a woman, Ellen Johnson-Sirleaf—was actively erecting barriers to stem the flow of small arms and promote the aims of the United Nations Programme of Action. Liberia was also tackling one of the major fallouts from the illicit flow of small arms by trying to create jobs in order to keep its children and youth from falling prey to charlatans, traffickers and demigods that were still looking for ways to drag the country back into war.

The Minister to the President Responsible for National Defense, Former Fighters and the Disabled of War of the Congo, Jacques Yvon Ndolou, said Africa was aware that it must face the scourge of illicit small arms and light weapons on a collective basis, as evidenced by the December 2000 signing of the Bamako Declaration. The proliferation of firearms was contagious and was a major cause of insecurity in Central Africa. During the 1993–1999 civil war and conflict in the Congo, approximately 74,000 weapons had been acquired by the militia. The country was doing its utmost to end the illicit circulation of firearms and implement the Programme of Action.

Considerable progress had been made to protect and maintain national security, he continued. Disarmament, demobilization and reintegration were an integral part of strengthening peace, political stability, security, national reconciliation and socio-economic reconstruction. From 2003–2005, some 17,371 weapons had been collected. A comprehensive demobilization and reintegration programme adopted on 14 February 2006 aimed to reintegrate 19,000 ex-combatants, and collect the equivalent of 10,000 weapons and munitions. In January 2006, the Congo and the International Monetary Fund (IMF) signed a $17 million agreement to support demobilization and reintegration programmes.

Cyrus T. Gituai, Permanent Secretary, Provincial Administration/Internal Security, Office of the President of Kenya, said that, despite global concern over armed violence, precipitated by illicit arms movement and use, there were still visible covert arms transfers to non-State actors in the Horn of Africa and the Great Lakes region. Those transfers fanned violence, eroded human development and seriously undermined peace efforts that the region had heavily invested in.

Citing the situation in Somalia as an example of how material and financial support to non-State actors undermined the consolidation of peace and security by the Transitional Federal Government, he appealed to the Conference to take note of the consequences of such activities and their impact on regional security and stability, especially in the context of transfer controls and support to non-State actors. He urged States to support the Somali people. In the absence of institutions of governance or administration in the country, security there would remain a "pipe dream" without international assistance.

Burkina Faso's representative, François Oubida, said success in implementing the Programme of Action would depend on international cooperation. African countries had, within their limits, done everything possible to eradicate the illicit trade of small arms and light weapons. However, limited resources made it difficult to accomplish that task. Burkina Faso had set up a commission to regularly follow up that progress and had established an annual budget to operate it. However, funding was insufficient and a serious handicap for the commission, given the subregion's many needs.

International partners must lend a hand, he said. The Programme of Action recognized that international cooperation and assistance by all stakeholders was a necessity. However, many international partners had not been very visible and had exhibited themselves very selectively. Although the road ahead would be long and the impediments many and sundry, Burkina Faso remained optimistic about making progress in the fight against illicit small arms and light weapons.

Boniface G. Chidyausiku of Zimbabwe, who spoke on behalf of the African Group, presented his delegation's position on the illicit trade in small arms and light weapons, which had been adopted by the 2005 Second Continental Conference of African Governmental Experts on the trade in Windhoek, Namibia. It had reaffirmed the landmark 2000 Bamako Declaration on the Illicit Proliferation, Circulation and Trafficking of Small Arms and Light Weapons and reiterated that both that Declaration and the Programme of Action were key to efforts to support conflict prevention and resolution, as well as sustainable post-conflict reconstruction and long-term peace and security.

He said the Conference had also requested that multilateral and regional institutions include provisions for small arms and light weapons programmes in post-conflict rehabilitation and reconstruction initiatives, in order to strengthen legislation and enhance the capacity of law enforcement agencies, among other things. Finally, while reaffirming the relevance of the Programme of Action, the Windhoek Conference had also requested that its integrity be maintained and that it should not be open to negotiation. It recommended that the Review Conference produce a report and set a date for a follow-up review no later than 2012, along with biennial meetings of States in 2008 and 2010.

The Minister for Foreign Affairs of Andorra also made a statement, as did the Deputy Ministers for Foreign Affairs of Nicaragua, Zambia and the Republic of Korea.

The Joint Secretary of Disarmament and International Security Affairs of the Ministry of External Affairs of India and the Deputy Inspector General for the Namibian Police of Namibia also made statements.

The Minister of the Interior of Mozambique, the Under-Secretary for Arms Control and International Security Affairs of the United States, the Deputy Minister for the Interior of Ghana, the

Deputy Director of the Department of Security and Disarmament of the Ministry of Foreign Affairs of the Russian Federation, the National Coordinator a.i. of the PFN/Democratic Republic of the Congo and Embassy First Counsellor in charge of the Political Division of Management of International Organizations of the Ministry for Foreign Affairs and International Cooperation of the Democratic Republic of the Congo, and the Deputy Director for Multilateral Affairs of the Department of Foreign Affairs of South Africa also made statements.

Also speaking were the representatives of Algeria (on behalf of the Arab Group), Belarus (on behalf of the Collective Security Treaty Organization), Lebanon, Bangladesh, Costa Rica, Venezuela, Viet Nam, Kyrgyzstan, Bolivia, Syria, Peru, Uruguay, Turkey, United Republic of Tanzania, Yemen, Israel, New Zealand and the Netherlands.

Globalization Makes Illicit Small Arms Trades Easier

Aditi Malhotra

In the following viewpoint, Aditi Malhotra argues the dangers of the illicit small arms trade. Malhotra contends that globalization helps the proliferation of illegal small arms, but countries can still take steps to prevent it. The sale of illicit small arms has had negative consequences in all nations, though some have suffered more than others. It is unlikely that the black market for guns could ever be entirely disbanded. Malhotra is a writer for the Toronto-based Geopolitical Monitor, an international intelligence publication.

As you read, consider the following questions:

1. How does globalization spur the small arms black market?
2. What is the Control Arms Campaign?
3. What makes combatting the illicit arms trade difficult?

I n June 2010, the representatives of all United Nations (UN) Member States came together at the Biennial Meeting of States in New York to consider the implementation of the 2001 Programme of Action (POA) on the illicit trade in small arms. The program was initiated in July 2001 to keep a check on the ever-growing illicit trade on Small Arms and Light Weapons (SALW) and to help countries, combat this pernicious problem. While the forum has worked continuously for the cause and attempts to achieve

"The Illicit Trade of Small Arms," by Aditi Malhotra, Geopoliticalmonitor Intelligence Corp., January 19, 2011. Reprinted by permission.

a certain degree of success in implementing the POA, there are numerous areas that still remain extremely challenging to deal with. Even though, the campaigns for combating illicit arms trade stirred reasonable support for the cause but largely, the progress has not been noteworthy. A few such disappointments can be incapability to act on setting international standards of marking and tracing of SALW and regulating illicit arms brokers.

While most of the issues relating to the illicit trade of SALW are highlighted in the media, few talk about ways and methods through which globalization has spurred the black market of SALW. It Is imperatively important to realize the magnitude of illicit activities that take place under the garb of globalization and work towards it comprehensively. Globalization is not new and neither is the black market. In the contemporary times, terrorism has been regarded as a major threat to world security. Intensive media coverage devoted to terrorism obscures other similar threats that haunt international security. Black market of arms and ammunitions is one of them. The illegal market for munitions encompasses top-of-the-line tanks, radar systems that detect Stealth aircraft, and the makings of the deadliest weapons of mass destruction. One prominent example in the history of arms black market is the sale of 87 Hughes helicopters to North Korea in the mid-1980s.

While the issue of global illicit trade of small arms does not attract much attention in the international arena, it evidently is an issue of pressing importance. The global illegitimate business in small arms is valued approximately around US$ 1 billion. Even though, the figure does not seem very outrageous, it's important to realize that it's the small arms that fuel crime and sustain armed conflicts world over, for example, 4 decades in Columbia and continues to plague the country of Afghanistan. It is equally responsible for facilitating terrorism and creating anarchy after civil wars. Burundi, Ghana, Yemen, Kyrgyzstan, Nepal, Pakistan are few of many countries that suffer from this form of "black globalization."

The structure of the small arms black market today is a complex network stretching across the globe, siphoning the gains of globalization. At heart, it's essential to map out the structure of illicit arms trade which not only includes black market, but also grey market and craft production.

The journey of small arms begins from the legal circuit and eventually falls into illegal clutches. There are multiple ways through which the legally originated arms get diverted to illegal spheres. Shipping through dangerous routes, stockpile mismanagement, loots, corruption among officials, warzone seizures are a few of them.

The World of Globalized Crime

Tom G. Palmer of the Cato Institute defines Globalization as "the diminution or elimination of state-enforced restrictions on exchanges across borders and the increasingly integrated and complex global system of production and exchange that has emerged as a result."[1]

The ideation of globalization advocates free market forces with minimized economic barriers and open trade for world development. This forms the basis of expansion of arms black market. With minimized custom regulations and border control, trafficking of small arms becomes easier. A miniscule percent of container ships have cargo checks, therefore making the arms movement smooth. Faking documents (bills of lading, forged end-use certificates),[2] bribing officials and concealing arms as humanitarian aids are common practices. In 2002, traffickers acquired 5,000 AK-47s from Yugoslavian army stocks and moved them from Serbia to Liberia under the guise of a legal transaction with Nigeria. One of the planes used in this shipment came from Ukraine and made a refueling stop in Libya while en route.[3]

Political and economic integration are coupled with lesser restrictions in migration and human movement. This helps the arms dealers to fortify their present business connections and tap new ones. Dealers migrate to various regions, motivated by business expansion or reduced operational risks. In case of arrests, arms dealers travel to countries where it is not possible to get extradited. The following case sheds some light on the argument. Abu Salem, an underworld criminal from India, who besides having a lengthy criminal record, was involved in providing illegal arms for 1993 serial bomb blasts in India. To escape arrest, he left for Portugal. After 3 years of legal disputes, Indian authorities managed to extradite Abu Salem from Lisbon, Portugal. It was after this case that India and Portugal signed an extradition treaty in 2007.

Further, banking reforms and capital mobility have aided the black market to spread its trade internationally, utilizing every angle of the well linked financial market. This also gives rise to offshore markets and tax shelters. An illustration of banking innovation is Emoney. Banks have introduced cards bearing microchips, which are able to store large sums of money. These cards are portable outside conventional channels or can be easily bartered among individuals. The money involved in illegal arms deals is exorbitant and the use of Emoney makes transactions easier.

The linkage of banks with the internet has posed a new challenge in combating illegitimate activities in the financial sector. E-banking has digitized money making it prone to criminality. Even though, it has numerous benefits for the world at large, it is misused for money laundering, credit card scams and check-kiting.[4] Adding to this, economic integration among regions blesses arm brokers with more opportunities to shelter their money, by investing in different stock exchanges. Numerous other illegal practices are a by-product of a deregulated financial sector, but money laundering is at the apex.

Money Laundering or "cleansing of money" is an unlawful practice of concealing the point of origin, identity or destination of the funds, when performing a particular financial transaction. The criminals maneuver money across borders gaining from banks in countries with lax anti-laundering policies.

Profound expansion of commercial airline and freight industry (making transport cheaper and easier) are instrumental in increased penetration of arms in conflict zones. Global merger of airline companies, supply chains, shipping firms make it tough to supervise unlawful practices in air and water.

The growth of global communication in the past two decades has been unfathomable. This has enhanced the ability of arms dealers to communicate internationally through the web at a cheap rate. Arms dealers use "cloned" cellular phones and unsecured broadband networks to surpass any chances of getting traced. Satellite phones are an option in remote areas where other means cannot be operated, providing an uninterrupted channel of contact and reach. Sometimes, arms deals are conducted through wires, where the privilege of anonymity prevails. In 2004, British police arrested more than 50 people in a series of raids to crack down criminals who bought illegal arms from abroad over the internet.[5]

Illicit arms trade is not isolated from other global illegal activities. When small arms flow to the black market, they become one of many illegal commodities there. The arms can be exchanged for money, drugs, conflict diamonds, endangered species etc. It becomes extremely tough to distinguish individual illegal acts in a web of transnational crime. Activities of arms dealers stretch across to other transnational criminal organizations (TCOs), like the drug and human traffickers, smugglers, terrorists', mafias etc. For instance, members of Al Qaeda hail from numerous countries, bearing fake passports and identities for security and ease of functioning. Their arms belong to black or grey markets ranging from Afghanistan, North West Pakistan, Uzbekistan, Latin America etc. Some arms were siphoned by ISI during the Soviet-Afghan war. Additionally, they also rely on profits incurred from drug trade originating in Afghanistan.

Global Governance

*United Nations (UN) Programme of Action to Prevent,
Combat and Eradicate the Illicit Trade in Small
Arms and Light Weapons in All Its Aspects.*

The UN initiated the Programme of Action after initial study on effect of small arms on the societies. In July 2001, UN conducted a conference on the Illicit Trade of SALW in All its Aspects. The conference focussed on the measures nations could take to combat the widespread problem of illicit arms trade. During this period, International Action Network on Small Arms (IANSA) took birth, which was an amalgamation of numerous NGOs. Today, IANSA has 700 members which are growing continuously.

The program bought the issue of the proliferation and abuse of SALW. It focuses on making illicit gun manufacturing a criminal act, destroying surplus arms, issuing end-user certificates for transfers, marking and tracing of guns, sharing information, documenting the records of gun production, imposing stricter enforcements on weapons sanctions.[6]

UN Firearms Protocol

Another program commenced by the UN was the UN Firearms Protocol, which came into effect from 3rd July 2005. This program was to supplement to the United Nations Convention against TCOs. The protocol seeks to encourage, assist and build up cooperation between states to combat illegal trafficking in SALW and monitoring its activities.

Till September 2005, 44 states approved the Protocol. A major problem that hinders in the success for this program is the acceptance of majority of the states. Its important to penetrate the will of the global community, so that the measures proposed in the program are effectively implemented and not in words.[7]

Control Arms Campaign and the Arms Trade Treaty

Control Arms is a global campaign launched in October 2003 by Amnesty International, Oxfam International and IANSA. It centers on the global trade of SALW and advocates against irresponsible transfers of arms to countries which practice human rights abuse. It clearly endorses striker arms trade laws which would prohibit the augmentation of grey market and black market.

Even after numerous efforts to do away with the illicit arms trade, there has not been any international treaty that binds countries into a common cause. The control arms campaign proposes an International Arms Trade Treaty (ATT). The ATT would be a legally binding treaty which would unite the country's present commitments under an international law. Presently, the treaty has the support of almost 153 countries and more that 800 NGO's.[8, 9]

International Criminal Police Organization (Interpol)

Interpol is an organization that facilitates cooperation of international police. It was established in 1923 and today enjoys a membership of 186 member states. It focuses on transnational crimes like terrorism, money laundering, drug, human and illicit arms trafficking etc.

Interpol has been aggressively involved in the illicit arms trade and have been tracing and tracking arms trafficking activities world over, with cooperation from its members. One of the admirable examples of their work is the arrest of Victor Bout, world's largest arms dealer, alleged of delivering weapons to Al Qaeda and the Taliban. The arrest was result of a multi-country operation.[10]

In 2006, Interpol was working on a study in collaboration with International Criminal Court, to launch a pilot project comprising of data collection and information analysis concerning primary figures involved in illicit arms brokering.[11]

Regional Level

Latin America and Caribbean

Major Problems:

- Increasing demand due to general increase in criminal and cross-border activities.

- Approximately 90% of illicit arms enter through Columbia, Panama and Guatemala

- Illicit homemade firearms post a challenge. They flow from Central and North America.

Regional efforts:

- Countries like Paraguay have toughened their small arms legislations and are cooperating to share information on the issue (member states of Mercosur).

- The United Nations Regional Centre for Peace, Disarmament and Development in Latin America and the Caribbean (UN-LIREC), the Organization of American States (OAS), and Mecosur are working towards supportive ventures to build small arms control programmes.

- Organizations from different regions are coming together to act. For example, Andean Community is coordinating with Nairobi Secretariat, SaferAfrica and EU for the cause.

- The Caribbean Community (Caricom) set up a ministerial body to counsel on small arms and seeks to launch a Weapons Intelligent Unit to trace arms within the region.

- OAS adopted the Inter-American Convention against the Illicit Manufacturing of and Trafficking in Firearms, Ammunition, Explosives, and Other Related Materials (CIFTA) in 1997, the first international treaty to target illegal arms trade.

The Pacific

Major Problems:

- SALW are readily available and there is a lack of control and regulation

- Availability of old stocks in the region

- Lack of infrastructure for stockpile management

Regional Efforts:

- Pacific Islands Forum Regional Security Committee (FRSC) has established processes for an effective regional approach to combat the problem by regular control, tracing the production, possessions etc.

- FRSC were instrumental in developing two important documents, namely, the Honiara initiative, Nadi Declaration (established framework of legislation to be used in national authority) and also the Biketawa Declaration (2001).

South East Asia

Major Problems:

- Illicit trafficking in SALW is causing instability and threatening security

- Number of intra-state conflicts that plague the region are instrumental in increasing the demand

- Long maritime regions are tough to monitor and national inventories are not managed properly.

Regional efforts:

- In 1999, the ASEAN Plan of Action to Combat Transnational Crime was adopted, which comprised a major section of illicit arms trafficking.

- Improvement in information flow and coordinated work between ASEAN Chiefs of National Police (ASEANPOL), customs and immigration officials facilitates better working.

- In May 2000, ASEAN focused exclusively on SALW, together with Indonesia, UN Regional Centre for Peace and Disarmament in Asia and the Pacific and Japan.

Sub Saharan Africa

Major Problems:

- Demand due to inter/intra state conflict and other ethnic and religious disputes.
- Firearms have fueled uncontained conflicts like Liberia, Congo etc.
- Slow progress in developing national and regional points of contact on the issue.

Regional efforts:

- The Southern African Development Community (SADC), the Economic Community of West African States (ECOWAS) and the Nairobi Secretariat have recognized national and regional divisions purposely regarding the illegal small arms trade.

- SADC and Nairobi Secretariat collaborated through lawfully binding understanding directed towards the eradication of the problem; Nairobi Secretariat is also jointly working with Eastern Africa Police Chiefs Cooperation Organization (EAPCCO) and Inter-Governmental Authority on Development (IGAD) on developing methods of control the trade.

- The Programme for Coordination and Assistance for Security and Development (PCASED), (ECOWAS + UN Development Programme) has supported 13 out of 15 ECOWAS Members to create commissions for the execution of ECOWAS Moratorium on Importation, Exportation and Manufacture of Light Weapons.

The Arab World

Major Problems:

- US-led invasion of Iraq added to the already high number of small arms in the region.

- The issue of Palestinian refugees and underdevelopment in the particular area have lead to increasing demands.

- Insufficient regulation of SALW holistically in the Arab world

Regional efforts:

- The League of Arab States is effectively monitoring the illegal activities related to small arms. The main point of concern for them is the Palestinian issue, which has given rise to the illegal arms trafficking and terrorism.

- In December 2003, the League and the UN Department for Disarmament Affairs (UNDDA) employed the UN Programme of Action in the region.

Europe

Major Problems:

- Major small arms exporters in the world hail from the Europe.

- Some countries have high levels of gun violence across the region, whereas some have very low levels.

- Uncontrolled proliferation of illicit trafficking in small arms in South-Eastern Europe.

Regional efforts:

- The illicit arms trade issue was initially given emphasis in OSCE in 1996, and established the OSCE document on SALW, guiding countries on national regulation, monitoring illegal brokering, export restriction, weapons destructions etc.

- The South Eastern Europe Clearinghouse for the Control of Small Arms and Light Weapons (SEESAC) is an important organisation in the struggle against illicit trade of SALW in

> South Eastern Europe, providing assistance and training to countries with lack of resources.

- Even though numerous steps have been taken at different levels, they have been unable to produce reasonable results. Although holistically viewed, the actions seem to be inadequate and ineffective.

National Level

Illicit arms trade is a threat to majority of countries in the world. The word limits makes it tough to trace national efforts taken by different countries. Primarily, all countries working towards this problem employ their national police service, administrative and bureaucratic services to combat the problem. The degree of devotion to the problem varies with countries majorly depending on the level of threat the problem poses to them.

Loopholes

- No internationally binding treaty to combat the problem.
- No agreed international standard of marking and tracing weapons.
- No transparency in arms export and transfer of arms to "high risk regions."
- Covert authorized arms transfers.
- Arms supply to non-state actors/embargoes countries.
- Lax custom policies or careless officials.
- No agreement/treat directly targeting the illegal arms brokers.

Recommendations

- Establish a common international standard of marking and tracing the SALW. This should be followed by all countries so that there is no discrepancy in the markings. If followed properly, this practice would make it easier to trace the illegal weapons and the routes from where they reach the wrong hands.

- Stipulate common paradigms of stockpile management and security. This would consequently make it easier for officials to minimize cases of stockpile loot. Adding to this, the practice of destroying surplus should be well promoted to avoid the arms reaching unlawful dealers.

- The governments should make arms licensing stricter and lesser available for the civil population and establish tougher requirements for attaining arms. Parallel to that, laws should be devised to monitor the activities of arms brokers and clearly lay down the boundaries of their role.

- National laws relating to illegal arms trade should be strengthened, regularly updated and reformed according to the progress and needs of the problem. The government should also control the activities of private companies within their jurisdiction. Private companies should be restricted to supply arms to states where slack law enforcements make it easier for illicit dealers to siphon arms.

- The present multilateral agreements should be strengthened. The most effective action can be taken at regional levels, as the agreements are flexible to the needs of each region. Therefore, the more multilateral and regional agreements should be worked upon through better cooperation, information sharing and strictly adhering to embargoes imposed on various regions.

- Arms sales should be regulated and monitored nationally and internationally and common international benchmarks of export practices should be ascertained for countries to act better and in coordination.

- Transparency is the most important factor for pursuing responsible exports. Presently, the exporters of arms hardly practice transparency. It is not just important to transfer arms to countries but to trace that the arms are in responsible hands and not abused for inhuman purposes or illegitimate practices.

- Lastly, it's significant and inevitably important to pave way towards an International Arms Trade Treaty. The ATT proposed is a well documented treaty containing majorly all aspects of arms trade. If the treaty is accepted internationally, then it would form the basis of a strong mechanism to restrict the irresponsible sale of SALW and reduce the negative effects that it has on the global society.

The Inevitability of the Black Market

After an extensive study on the illicit arms trade and its global governance, it is important to see the dark side of the same coin. It's a universal perception that governmental actions, multilateral coordination and stricter laws would bring an end to this curse. Unfortunately, this is not true. The black market survives on the simple rules of economics where market forces dominate the game. Guns are illegal today, but there are people (terrorists, individuals, rebel groups etc.) who desire it. Consequently, this creates the demand. In order to satiate the demand, there needs to be a supplier. Supplying guns (which is an illegal act) involves a lot of risk because of the coercive actions of the state. In normal circumstances, this would be too perilous, but there is a catch. The people who demand SALW are ready to pay a higher price than the legal price. Therefore, this scenario gets the suppliers a heavy profit by taking the risk. Over a period of time, the supplier becomes adept in their work and finds new means to get new arms, whether they are by siphoning from legal market, looting from stockpiles or accumulating abandoned guns from conflict zones. With unbound profits from for each deal, the suppliers become richer and stronger.

Even with stricter laws and embargoes, the demand would remain. Now satisfying the demand means greater risk, which implies a higher price for the same gun. This in turn means higher profit for the dealers.[12] This clearly reflects that the black market would never get eliminated. The only way to abolish this is to abolish the demand. This is best explained by Aaron Karp, "To eliminate the gray market would require universal acceptance of the political status quo, the end of international politics. Short of world government or a powerful system of collective security, states will continue to find the appeal of the gray market to be irresistible."[13] In the nutshell, the future of black markets depends on the events of this globalized world which can either boost illicit trade or cripple it to an insignificant level.

Notes

[1] Tom G. Palmer, 'Globalization Is Grrrreat!', Cato Institute 1:2-6, < http://www.cato.org/pubs/letters/palmer-catoletters.pdf>, 2002.

[2] End-Use Certificate, in shipping, a document intended to assure authorities of the eventual application (generally also the final customer and destination) of a particular actual or intended shipment. End-use certificates are needed in cases in which there are political controls on exports, such as advanced military weapons, MSN Encarta, < http://encarta.msn.com/encyclopedia_762505541/end-use_certificate.html>.

[3] Rachel Stohl, 'The Tangled Web of Illicit Arms Trafficking', Centre for American Progress p. 21, <http://www.americanprogress.org/issues/2004/10/b217737.html>, 2004.

[4] Check kiting is a form of fraud involving the sloshing of theoretical funds between two bank checking accounts. A check written to the criminal from one bank is deposited, and more importantly credited, to an account at a second bank. Because that second bank now shows a positive balance, the criminal can withdraw enough money to deposit back into the first bank before the check bounces for lack of funds, Wisegeek, <http://www.wisegeek.com/what-is-check-kiting.htm>.

[5] 'British police arrest over 50 for acquiring illegal arms via internet', People's Daily Online, 1 July, 2004, <http://english.peopledaily.com.cn/200407/01/eng20040701_148103.html>.

[6] All the information in this section is abridged from the IANSA homepage > Specifically, the data was available in the section of UN Programme of Action on Small Arms and Light Weapons.

[7] All the information in this section is abridged from the UN Office of Drugs and Crime homepage.

[8] The information in the 1st and 2nd paragraphs is abridged form data available at the Control Arms homepage.

[9] Debbie Hillier & Brian Wood, 'Shattered Lives: the case for tough international arms control'. Amnesty International and Oxfam International, Control Arms, p. 76 2003.

[10] 'INTERPOL praises international co-operation behind arrest of suspected international arms dealer by Thai Paolice' INTERPOL media release, 7 March. 2008.

[11] The information was abridged from 'Need for Global Action to Combat Illicit Arms Brokering Highlighted, as Preparatory Meeting for Small Arms Conference Continues', United Nations Information Service, , 2006.

[12] The idea reflected in this section is largely based on the following article. Curt Bolding, 'The Layman's Guide to Black Market Firearms', 2AMPD, <http://www.2ampd.net/Articles/Bolding/The_Layman's_Guide_to_Black_Market_Firearms.htm> , 2000.

[13] Aaron Karp, 'The Rise of Black and Gray Markets', American Academy of Political and Social Science, <http://www.jstor.org/stable/pdfplus/1048134.pdf>.

Periodical and Internet Sources Bibliography

The following articles have been selected to supplement the diverse views presented in this chapter.

"Arms Trade Key Statistics," BBC News, 15 September 2005, http://news.bbc.co.uk/2/hi/business/4238644.stm.

Saeed Kamali Dehghan, "Global Arms Trade Reaches Highest Point Since Cold War Era," *Guardian*, February 19, 2017, https://www.theguardian.com/world/2017/feb/20/global-arms-weapons-trade-highest-point-since-cold-war-era.

Barry Kolodkin, "What Is Arms Control?" Thoughtco, March 18, 2017, https://www.thoughtco.com/what-is-arms-control-3310297.

Charlie May, "Trump Plans to Greatly Expand Arms Sales Around the World," Salon, January 8, 2018 https://www.salon.com/2018/01/08/trump-plans-to-greatly-expand-arms-sales-around-the-world/.

Sanjana Sharma, Cyber Security for the Defence Industry, Cyber Security Review, http://www.cybersecurity-review.com/industry-perspective/cyber-security-for-the-defence-industry/.

Anna Stavrianakis, "Parliament Urgently Needs to Keep Tabs on Britain's Arms Exports," The Conversation, January 14, 2016, https://theconversation.com/parliament-urgently-needs-to-keep-tabs-on-britains-arms-exports-52865."The Rise and Fall of Global Arms Sales," World Economic Forum, October 4 2017, https://www.weforum.org/agenda/2017/10/the-rise-and-fall-of-global-arms-sales.

"Weapons and Markets, Small Arms Survey," http://www.smallarmssurvey.org/weapons-and-markets.html.

GLOBALVIEWPOINTS

CHAPTER 2

The Effects of the Arms Trade

The Arms Trade Treaty Attempts to Regulate International Arms Transfers

Amnesty International

After decades of work on behalf of activists and governments, the Arms Trade Treaty (ATT) was ratified in 2014. Amnesty International was a supporter of the ATT. Amnesty International and other organizations recognize that poor regulation of arms sales results in a great number of civilian casualties and injuries. The ATT also seeks to end the sale of weapons to parties who would use them to commit genocide or war crimes. Amnesty International is a non-government organization focusing on human rights.

As you read, consider the following questions:

1. Why was the Arms Trade Treaty created?
2. Why does the ATT call for transparency in arms deals?
3. What are some conditions that ban the sale of weapons under the ATT?

The global Arms Trade Treaty (ATT), created to rein in the poorly regulated international arms transfers that fuel war crimes and serious human rights abuses, will face its first major test in Mexico this week, Amnesty International said today.

The ATT's first Conference of States Parties, taking place in Cancún from 24–27 August, will be attended by dozens of states, including some that have neither signed nor ratified the treaty since its adoption in 2013. Amnesty International, which campaigned alongside NGO partners for more than two decades to make the ATT a reality, will also attend the meeting.

"Cancún marks the first major test for the Arms Trade Treaty, and states will have an important opportunity to make history by following through on the treaty's lifesaving goals," said Marek Marczynski, Head of Military, Security and Police at Amnesty International.

"We'll be making sure the talks don't get bogged down in bureaucracy or lose sight of the ATT's guiding principles—effective and transparent regulation to end the human suffering caused by irresponsible flows of conventional arms."

Three major areas Amnesty International will be pressing for are:

- transparency in all aspects of the ATT, including comprehensive state reporting on the scale and range of their arms imports and exports;

- making sure NGOs are allowed to participate meaningfully in all treaty meetings and processes; and

- putting in place mechanisms to ensure that states honor their treaty obligations by preventing transfers of weapons to anyone who risks using them for serious violations of international law, including war crimes and other serious human rights violations.

Transparency is one of the ATT's main objectives since the global trade in arms has, up until now, been shrouded in secrecy. It is also a key means of demonstrating that States are implementing the treaty, and will help to assess how the ATT is being applied in practice.

During the run-up to the Mexico conference, discussions in preparatory meetings focused on the ongoing participation of civil society groups, as well as how much information on arms imports and exports states should report and make publicly available.

Some states are trying to curb the role of civil society by significantly restricting their participation in future ATT conferences and making an increasing number of key decisions behind closed doors in secret sessions.

Amnesty International is also alarmed that states have attempted to strip their ATT reporting requirements down to a bare minimum. This means that they may only be obliged to report on the financial value of transfers annually, without providing crucial details about the size of the shipment, the number of items and an accounting of each category of small arms and light weapons included.

Details about where the weapons would end up and for what purpose would also be secret, which is crucial information aimed at preventing diversion of arms into illicit markets and to unauthorized end users.

"Shutting civil society out of some of the most important discussions and not making annual reports on arms imports and exports public will mean "business as usual"—arms transfers will remain shrouded in secrecy, undermining the purpose of the ATT. This must not be allowed to happen," said Marek Marczynski.

"A great deal has been achieved through the work of civil society alongside States to win legally binding, global rules on international arms transfers. We look forward to continue playing a constructive role as we move into the implementation phase. States must adopt comprehensive and transparent reporting requirements that give a full picture of the global trade in arms."

Background

Since the early 1990s Amnesty International has campaigned with NGO partners to achieve robust, legally binding, global rules on international arms transfers to stem the flow of conventional arms and munitions that fuel atrocities and human rights abuses. More than a million people around the world joined the campaign.

On 2 April 2013, a total of 155 states voted in the UN General Assembly to adopt the Arms Trade Treaty. It entered into force as binding international law on 24 December 2014, for all states parties.

Five of the top 10 arms exporters—France, Germany, Italy, Spain and the UK—are among the 72 states around the world to have already ratified the ATT. The USA, by far the largest arms producer and exporter, is among 58 other countries that have signed but not yet ratified the treaty. Other major arms producers like China, Canada and Russia have resisted signing or ratifying the treaty.

The ATT includes a number of robust rules to stop the flow of arms to countries when it is known the arms would be used for genocide, crimes against humanity or war crimes. Governments that are part of the ATT will now have to carry out objective assessments to avoid an overriding risk that an arms export would be used to commit serious violations of international human rights law or international humanitarian law.

International arms transfers are shrouded in secrecy but the value of the global trade is estimated to be approaching US$100 billion annually.

Amnesty International has continued to document and expose irresponsible arms transfers that contribute to or facilitate grave abuses.

This includes weapons and ammunition predominantly manufactured in the Russian Federation/former Soviet Union, Belarus, Ukraine and China transferred to Sudan, and subsequently used by all sides of the conflicts in South Kordofan and Darfur as well as neighboring South Sudan. In South Kordofan, Amnesty International has recently documented a series of indiscriminate attacks on civilian areas, including hospitals and schools, of a nature and scale that constitute war crimes and possibly crimes against humanity.

In Iraq and Syria, rampant arms proliferation has seen arms transfers being diverted to the armed group calling itself Islamic

State and other armed groups. These arms are being used to facilitate summary killings, enforced disappearances, rape and torture, amongst other serious human rights violations. The spread of arms and ammunition—mostly Soviet/Warsaw Pact-era small arms and light weapons, armored vehicles and artillery dating back to the 1970s and 80s—has caused untold impact on the civilian population, creating large flows of internally displaced peoples and refugees, impeding access to humanitarian assistance and exacerbating gender-based violence.

We Can Learn from the Sale of Weapons After the Cold War

International Committee of the Red Cross

In the following excerpted viewpoint, which comes from a study done close to twenty years ago, the International Committee of the Red Cross argues that history has taught us important lessons regarding arms sales. While the political landscape has changed greatly since this report was published, it is important for readers to understand the effect of arms deals on civilians. The end of the Cold War and the collapse of the former Soviet Union provide a tragic case study on the true costs arms deals have on human life. The International Committee of the Red Cross (ICRC) helps people affected by conflict and armed violence and promotes the laws that protect victims of war.

As you read, consider the following questions:

1. What percentage of those injured in armed combat are thought to be civilians?
2. What effect were large scale arms sales thought to have had in Rwanda in 1994?
3. What makes small arms particularly popular in combat?

With the end of the Cold War and the collapse of the former Soviet Union, the pattern of both conflict and international arms transfers[2] has changed significantly. These changes have contributed to creating high levels of civilian casualties and an extremely difficult environment for the delivery of humanitarian assistance. Although the present study focuses primarily on the role of arms availability, an understanding of the relationship between the availability of weapons and the nature of armed conflict in the 1990s is essential to a proper analysis of the problem at hand. Although arms may increase the lethality of conflicts and facilitate aggression against civilian populations many other factors contribute to the heavy toll paid by civilians in recent conflicts.

A Proliferation of Actors and a Diversity of Motives

In the 1990s, the nature of armed conflict has changed dramatically. The withdrawal of superpower support has compelled armed groups and governments to become increasingly self-reliant to ensure their own survival—whether by selling weapons abroad or by associating political and military efforts with commercial pursuits. For insurgent groups in particular this "privatization" of armed struggle has meant trading, often illegally, in resources under their control. As such groups already operate outside the law, illegal trade can give them a comparative advantage over other dealers—whether the product sold is diamonds, ivory, narcotics, wood products or weapons. The transactions are easier when there is little or no State control in areas of rebel influence and where transborder cooperation with friendly populations or governments in neighboring countries is possible.

When trade in local resources is not an option, insurgents often turn for support, through violence or threats of violence, to the local population and international humanitarian agencies, which are sometimes forced to turn over goods and materials intended for aid operations. In such situations the possession of arms can become a *sine qua non* for subsistence, whether one is part of an insurgent force or a local peasant. The "privatization" of security has also led to a decentralization of command and control over armed forces. Since resources are not provided by an external patron[3] or perhaps even by the leaders of insurgent movements, the chain of command essential for maintaining discipline in armed forces also tends to break down. Power, authority and well-being derive not from a central source but from the arms cache, drug route or mineral deposit one controls, on the degree of fear that can be instilled in the local population or on the amount of material that can be siphoned off from international agencies. In this context it is easy to imagine a proliferation of armed groups the identities of which are difficult to discern. While these actors may also harbor political ambitions, their activities are frequently a strange and chaotic mix between armed struggle, illegal commerce and intimidation.

Another aspect of recent conflicts has been fighting along tribal, religious and ethnic lines. As State structures have eroded in many countries groups involved in combat of this nature have felt the need to protect themselves against real or perceived threats from other groups, central authorities or both. This type of conflict is mostly fought in and against local communities rather than against military targets. When the parties pursue policies such as "ethnic cleansing" the goal is no longer to put enemy troops hors de combat[4] but to drive civilians from their homes by terror, forced displacement, killings or a combination of all these. The intense hatred bred by such conflicts can bitterly divide societies, neighbors and even families long after the armed conflict itself has ended. The typical victims of such conflicts are precisely the civilians who are entitled to comprehensive protection under international humanitarian law.

In situations where the concept of respect for civilians and the vulnerable is not understood or is intentionally ignored, the principle of giving humanitarian workers access to those in need of assistance is often blatantly disregarded. In the words of one senior ICRC official: "There is no comparison (...) between the dangers to which ICRC delegates are exposed today and those they used to encounter in more traditional contexts. Because they are undesirable witnesses, because their activities slow down or even thwart the objectives of combatants, because they are "rich" in countries that are poor, for all these reasons delegates are considered perfectly legitimate targets by those who prey on humanitarian organizations."[5]

Civilian Casualties

Concern about the widespread availability of arms is driven by the misuse of weapons. Most of those who wish to understand the issues related to weapons availability and misuse have understandably focused on the occurrence of weapon injuries among the civilian population.

Over recent years a number of sources have cited figures that purport to document the proportion of civilians injured by weapons in various conflicts. Many of these sources put the proportion at 80 to 90% of all people injured. It is important to note that these estimates are almost always provided with no indication of how they have been arrived at. Most commonly, a reference is given which merely refers to an earlier report quoting the same figure. Thus, in recent years, a large number of documents by non-governmental organizations, international organizations, and even articles in the peer-reviewed medical literature have cited figures which are increasingly being used as "evidence" by those concerned with weapons availability and misuse, but which are difficult, if not impossible, to substantiate.

The figure of 80 to 90% may conceivably be correct in some circumstances. Logic alone would suggest that conflicts which are predominantly based on religious, ethnic, or cultural divisions do generate high levels of civilian casualties. However, these same conflict situations tend to be those without a sustained international presence, and estimating the number of individuals killed or wounded, let alone determining their combat status, is either not done, or relegated to educated guesswork.

Thus, despite concern about civilian weapon injury, there are relatively few sources that provide original data which directly addresses the issue. One such source is the ICRC surgical database, begun in 1991 to record information relating to the ICRC's surgical activities. An analysis of the first 17,086 people admitted for

2015 Arms Conference in Mexico

The inaugural Conference of State Parties, taking place in Cancun from August 24–27, will follow the lead of the global Arms Trade Treaty (ATT)—which was adopted in 2013 but still awaits implementation by world powers.

The ATT aims to regulate the international weapons industry through what the European Union describes as "greater responsibility and transparency." Many of the state representatives attending the conference have yet to sign or ratify the treaty.

"Cancún marks the first major test for the Arms Trade Treaty, and states will have an important opportunity to make history by following through on the treaty's lifesaving goals," said Amnesty International's Marek Marczynski.

The ATT must be fully implemented to prevent weapons from crossing through the black market and ending up "in the wrong hands," the EU said in a statement. This week's conference presents the first "opportunity to lay solid foundations for the ATT regime, by notably adopting its rules of procedure and financial rules, agreeing [to] common reporting arrangements and establishing the ATT Secretariat."

Oscar Arias Sanchez, former President of Costa Rica and Nobel Peace Prize winner, said the conference gives international actors an opportunity to speak for victims of the arms trade. "When weapons are circulating freely into the worst possible hands, the law must speak. When the lives of the innocent are placed in danger by an absence of regulation, the law must speak," he wrote in an op-ed published on Common Dreams this week. "And we must speak, today—in favor of this crucial treaty, and its swift and effective implementation. If we do, then when today's children of conflict look to us for guidance and leadership, we will no longer look away in shame."

"[N]o sane definition of national sovereignty includes the right to sell arms for the violation of human rights in other countries," Sanchez wrote. "A nation willing to carry out such an act is not defending itself, but rather infringing upon the sovereignty of other nations that only want to live in peace."

Only 72 countries have ratified the ATT thus far, including France, Germany, Italy, Spain, and the UK—some of the world's top arms exporters.

"Arms Conference in Mexico Aims to Bring Transparency to Weapons Trade," by Nadia Prupis, Common Dreams, August 24, 2015.

weapon injuries reported that 35% were female, males under 16, or males aged 50 and over.[6] Clearly, this figure is a conservative indicator of the proportion of people injured by weapons who were probably non-combatants[7] and who received care under the auspices of the ICRC. A study in Croatia used death certificates and employment records to examine the civilian proportion of conflict-related fatalities and found that civilians could at most have accounted for 64% of the 4,339 fatalities studied.[8]

Irrespective of which proportion of civilian casualties is felt to be most valid, there are a number of points that should be borne in mind. Firstly, all of the figures cited above suggest that civilian death and injury in recent armed conflicts is high given the protection to which civilians are entitled under international humanitarian law. Secondly, there is evidence that the proportion has been increasing over the course of the twentieth century.[9] Finally, concern over the "true" proportion of civilian casualties may be overly simplistic and somewhat misleading. To address the civilian population's needs in terms of protection during armed conflict, it is also necessary to examine the circumstances surrounding weapon injuries inflicted upon civilians, as is done in Section III. Consideration of the context of death or injury reveals differing injury mechanisms in specific situations, with very different implications for humanitarian intervention.[10]

Awash in Weapons

The Cold War competition between two strategic alliances, in which arms were made available primarily for global political and strategic purposes, has largely disappeared. Major weapons transfers by the principal exporting States are now often motivated primarily by economic and employment benefits. Military, strategic and political factors have become secondary considerations in many instances and are sometimes completely ignored. The human costs of arms transfers have, until recently, been considered of little importance.

A major impetus driving arms sales to developing States has been the rapidly shrinking military budgets of northern industrialized countries. The lack of coherent policies for conversion of military production capacities to serve the civilian economy has meant that military industries with high production capabilities generated by the Cold War are competing intensively to develop new markets, particularly in the developing world.

Even the former Czechoslovakia, which made a political decision in the early 1990s to cease arms exports, subsequently chose to re-enter the business for economic and other reasons. In addition, large quantities of surplus weapons have been transferred from the northern hemisphere to developing countries in the form of direct aid, subsidized sales or intra-alliance transfers. Ironically, these surplus arms are the by-product not only of reduced military budgets and forces in the industrialized countries but also of successful arms control agreements that have required members of NATO and the former Warsaw Pact to eliminate hundreds of thousands of weapons from their inventories.

This flow of surplus arms is not likely to end soon—unless preventive action is taken without delay. In the coming five to ten years a new wave of surplus weapons and ammunition into developing countries can be expected to result from the need for funds in some States of the former Soviet Union and the modernization of arsenals in countries slated to join NATO or those aspiring to do so.

Large-scale arms transfers can be a source of tension in peacetime and generate high levels of casualties once hostilities begin. Massive arms exports to Iraq throughout the 1980s are seen by many observers as having emboldened Iraq's incursion into Kuwait and as justifying the allied response in the second Gulf War (1990–1991). Arms transfers into Rwanda as tensions increased in 1994 and early 1995 are widely considered to have encouraged and facilitated the 1995 genocide in that country.[11] The effects of Cold War era arms transfers have been felt in numerous intrastate conflicts around the world.

On the national level, one of the dominant features of the post-Cold War period has been the breakdown in dozens of countries of the structures responsible for controlling arms availability. From the former Soviet republics to regions of conflict in the developing world, recent years have seen a melting away both of government structures capable of containing violence and of social norms which support tolerance and social cohesion. In a vicious cycle, arms availability creates a demand for yet more weapons as insecure groups and individuals arm themselves for protection and are at the same time seen as a threat by others. Each additional incident or atrocity confirms these perceptions.

Major Weapons Systems

In the late 1990s the trade in major conventional weapons, though drastically reduced, still accounts for tens of billions of dollars annually. At the same time the proliferation of small arms and light weapons appears to have increased, as indicated below. This is taking place in an environment where even the loose discipline previously imposed by the US and Soviet Union on their allies and client States has largely disappeared. In today's world of internal conflicts and civil strife accountability is much more difficult to impose and is often non-existent. The availability of weapons is increasingly governed by the laws of supply and demand with little or no regard to the behaviour of recipients. In the current "buyers market" suppliers, whether States or companies, are notably reluctant to condition sales on the behaviour or purposes of belligerents.

For many years now, the global trade in major conventional weapons (such as tanks, fighter aircraft, naval ships and armoured personnel carriers) has been documented by organizations such as the Stockholm International Peace Research Institute (SIPRI), the US Arms Control and Disarmament Agency, and more recently, the UN Register of Conventional Arms. The sale or transfer of these weapons in the 1970s and 1980s, both among NATO and Warsaw Pact members and from these alliances to developing countries, was relatively easy to track in terms of both trade flows and dollar amounts. Over time, the international community became increasingly concerned that the proliferation of major weapon systems was fuelling regional arms races that could break out into open warfare (e.g., the Iran-Iraq war of the 1980s).

The end of the Cold War was followed by a dramatic fall in global exports of major weapons systems, from a high of $40.5 billion in 1984 to $20 billion in 1994 (with a recent increase to $25 billion in 1997).[12, 13] In the developing world, economic constraints and the loss of favourable terms of credit from the superpowers to finance arms sales have resulted in similar reductions in arms imports, from $31 billion in 1987 to $12 billion in 1994 (with an increase to $18 billion in 1997).[14, 15] A significant development since the 1980s has been the emergence among developing countries of a number of new exporters of major weapons systems.

Small Arms and Light Weapons

While major weapons systems such as tanks and aircraft undoubtedly continue to account for many combatant and civilian deaths in ethnic and sectarian conflicts, the distinguishing features of small arms and light weapons have made them particularly well-suited to the intrastate conflicts of the 1990s, as explained below.

- Simplicity and durability: Unlike major weapons systems which require regular upkeep and maintenance due to their complicated electronics, avionics and propulsion subsystems, small arms and light weapons have few moving parts, are extremely durable and require little upkeep or logistical support. With minimal maintenance some items such as assault rifles can remain operational for 20 to 40 years or more. These weapons are widely used in conflicts involving uneducated combatants and children, because they are easy to handle effectively with a minimum of training.

- Portability and concealability: Small arms and light weapons can be carried by individuals or light vehicles; they are easily transported or smuggled into areas of conflict; and they can be concealed in shipments of legitimate cargo.

- Military/police and civilian uses: unlike major conventional weapons, which are generally procured only by national military forces, small arms and light weapons often have legitimate uses for both military and police forces. They may also be held, legally or otherwise, by individuals fearful for their own personal security.

- Low cost and wide availability: Because these weapons are mass manufactured for military, police and civilian use, there is an abundance of suppliers around the world. In addition, the existence of many tens of millions of such weapons, often recycled from conflict to conflict, has in many countries caused prices to drop well below the cost of manufacture. For example, a 1996 report indicated that in Mozambique and Angola an assault rifle could be purchased for less than $15 or for a bag of maize. In Uganda the price was reported to be the same as that of a chicken.[16]

- Lethality: The increasing sophistication of rapid-fire assault rifles, pistols and submachine guns, and their widespread circulation among sub-State groups and civilians, can provide such groups with firepower which matches or exceeds that of national police or even military forces. Indeed, with weapons capable of firing up to 700 rounds a minute, a single individual or small armed group can pose a tremendous threat to society. The development of new technologies for rocket-propelled grenades, mortars and light antitank weapons has increased the firepower that warring factions can bring to bear in a civil conflict.

In most conflicts of the 1990s death and injury have resulted less from the major conventional weapons associated with war (tanks, aircraft, warships) than from small arms and light weapons. The global proliferation of assault rifles, machine guns, mortars, rocket-propelled grenades, and so forth (i.e., weapons that can be carried by individuals, small groups or light vehicles) has facilitated the resort to armed violence in preference to political solutions.

A study of 101 conflicts fought between 1989 and 1996 revealed that small arms and light weapons were generally the weapons of preference or even the only weapon used.[17] Another study estimated that 3.2 million deaths occurred in internal armed conflicts during the period 1990-1995 alone.[18]

[...]

Notes

2. The term 'arms transfers', as defined in UN resolutions, refers to all arms or weapon systems transferred outside the control of the producing State. The term is broader than 'arms trade' in that it includes not only commercial sales but also changes of weapon ownership under aid programmes, exchanges of arms under military alliances and other non-monetary arrangements.

3. Nonetheless, in some cases armed militias have been financed by private companies to defend the companies' own interests.

4. i.e., out of action.

5. Jean-Daniel Tauxe, ICRC Director of Operations, Presentation to the ICRC Group of International Advisors, Geneva, September 1998.

6. D.R. Meddings. "Are Most Casualties Non-Combatants?," *British Medical Journal*, Vol. 317, 31 October 1998, pp. 1249–1250.

7. The ICRC does not normally ask the status of those seeking medical assistance.

8. M. Kuzman, B. Tomic, R. Stevanovic et al., "Fatalities in the War in Croatia, 1991 and 1992: Underlying and External Causes of Death," *JAMA*, 1993; 270:626–628.

9. R.M. Garfield and A.I Neugut, "Epidemiologic Analysis of Warfare: An Historical Review," JAMA, 1991, 266:688–692.

10. D.R. Meddings and S.M. O'Connor, "Weapons in Cambodia: Who is Injured and How?," *British Medical Journal*, in press.

11. Some commentators cite the fact that thousands of persons were killed in Rwanda by machetes to suggest the futility of limitations on the availability of even more lethal light weapons. However, these arguments overlook the fact that the killings were often facilitated by the rounding up and detention of civilians at gunpoint. Without these more sophisticated weapons large numbers of civilians might have been able to flee.

12. *SIPRI Yearbook* 1998, Stockholm International Peace Research Institute, Stockholm, 1998, pp. 291 & 294. Figures are in constant 1990 US dollars. It should be noted that these figures represent standardized trend indicators developed by SIPRI and do not necessarily reflect the actual costs paid.

13. Despite the changes in the overall volume of arms transfers the major weapons exporting countries have remained largely the same; between 1993 and 1997, these were (in order of volume) the USA, Russia, the United Kingdom, France, Germany, China, the Netherlands, Italy, Canada and Spain. Source: *ibid.*, p. 294.

14. *Ibid.*, p. 318, and SIPRI *Yearbook* 1993, p. 476 (figures also in constant 1990 US dollars).

15. The top twelve importing countries in the developing world have remained largely the same; between 1993 and 1997 these were (in order of volume) Saudi Arabia, Turkey, Egypt, South Korea, China, India, Kuwait, the United Arab Emirates, Thailand, Malaysia, Pakistan and Iran. Source: *op.cit.* (note 12), p. 300.

16. *Small Arms Management and Peacekeeping in Southern Africa*, United Nations Institute for Disarmament Research, Geneva (UNIDIR/96/21), 1996, p. 9.
17. P. Wallensteen and M. Sollenberg, "Armed Conflicts, Conflict Termination and Peace Agreements, 1989- 1996," *Journal of Peace Research*, Vol. 34, No. 3.
18. R. Legard Sivard, *World Military and Social Expenditures 1996*, World Priorities, Washington DC, 1996.

Are the Geneva Conventions Still Relevant?

Knut Dörmann

In the following viewpoint, in a question-answer format, Knut Dörmann argues the relevancy of the Geneva Conventions, the laws governing how nations act during wars between nations. The Geneva Conventions do not have rules for what is allowable during civil unrest. However, they do have rules to protect civilians during times of civil unrest. Negotiated over 150 years ago, the treaties may or may not be able to stand up to a changing conflict landscape. Dörmann is head of the International Committee of the Red Cross (ICRC) Legal Division.

As you read, consider the following questions:

1. What is the purpose of the Geneva Conventions?
2. How did the Geneva Convention change after World War II?
3. Why should war have limits?

On 12 August, 2009 the Geneva Conventions will turn 60—an important milestone for the treaties, which place limits on how war is waged and form the cornerstone of international humanitarian law (IHL).

In 1949, States met in Geneva to revise the existing Geneva Conventions and add a fourth one dedicated to the protection of civilians. Since then, these treaties have been supplemented by three Additional Protocols.

Some critics have suggested that the Conventions are approaching the age of retirement and are no longer suited for the kind of contemporary wars that pit regular armies against armed groups, and in an era when most wars are fought within States, not between them.

Proponents maintain that the rules are indeed still relevant and that the Conventions, together with their Additional Protocols, continue to provide the best available framework for protecting civilians and people who are no longer fighting.

What Are the Geneva Conventions and What Purpose Do They Serve?

The Conventions are the most important component of international humanitarian law, or IHL, as it is commonly known—the body of rules that protect civilians and people who are no longer fighting, including wounded and sick military personnel and prisoners of war. Their purpose is not to stop war but rather to limit the barbarity of armed conflict.

The Geneva Conventions only apply to international armed conflicts, with the exception of Article 3 common to all four Conventions, which also covers non-international armed conflicts. The adoption of this article in 1949 was a breakthrough since previous IHL treaties had only covered situations of wars between States. As most of today's wars are non-international armed conflicts, Article 3 remains vitally important because it sets a baseline for the protection of people who are not or no longer fighting, to which all sides—State and non-State parties to conflict—must abide.

Remarkably, the Conventions have been universally ratified, meaning every single State in the world is party to them. (States Party to the Geneva Conventions)

What Is the ICRC's Link to the Conventions?

The ICRC has been closely linked to the Geneva Conventions from the start. The founder of the ICRC, Henry Dunant, also had the idea for the First Geneva Convention, " for the amelioration of the condition of the wounded in armies in the field, " which was adopted in 1864.

Since Dunant's time, the ICRC has always tried to compare the Geneva Conventions, and IHL as a whole, to the reality of armed conflict as we experience it on the ground. From the very beginning, we have been part of a dynamic process which ensures that IHL is adapted to ongoing changes in warfare.

For example, in the years leading up to the Second World War, the ICRC drafted and sought approval for an International Convention on the condition and protection of civilians of enemy nationality who were on a territory belonging to or occupied by a belligerent. No action was taken on that text since governments refused to convene a diplomatic conference to decide on its adoption.

As a result, there was no specific treaty that protected civilians against the horrors of the Second World War. In response, the international community agreed in 1949 to adopt the Fourth Geneva Convention for the protection of civilians. This was really a watershed moment in terms of ensuring that civilian populations and property are spared during times of armed conflict.

Today, the ICRC derives its humanitarian mandate—its job description, in a sense—from the Conventions, which task the ICRC with visiting prisoners, organizing relief operations, re-uniting separated families and similar humanitarian activities during armed conflicts. The ICRC is mentioned explicitly in several provisions of the Conventions.

Some say that the Conventions were designed for a completely different world, and are now in need of being revised, if not rewritten. What's your response?

In my mind, the problem doesn't lie with the law. In fact, the Conventions have proven to be surprisingly relevant over the past six decades. Since 1949, the Conventions have been supplemented by the Additional Protocols and by important developments in customary international humanitarian law, which further strengthened the protection of civilians, especially in non-international armed conflicts, thus adapting to new realities.

The major challenge is that the law is not being respected nearly enough. Too few people know what the Geneva Conventions are, while too many warring parties ignore or flout them. I firmly believe that if the existing rules were respected and abided by, much of the suffering caused by current armed conflicts could be avoided.

At the same time, let's not forget that the Conventions have been hugely successful over the past 60 years, saving countless lives, allowing thousands of separated families to be reunited and providing comfort to millions of prisoners of war. In my mind, that's ample reason to celebrate. I dread to think how much more suffering there would be in the world if they didn't exist.

Let's also not forget that international armed conflicts and occupation are by no means a thing of the past. Last year's war between Russia and Georgia is a recent example of an international armed conflict where all four of the Geneva Conventions were applicable.

In what ways has IHL developed over the past six decades?

IHL has expanded considerably as the character and impact of war have evolved over the years. Notably, in 1977, two Additional Protocols were adopted. Additional Protocol I strengthened the protection of victims of international armed conflicts, while

Additional Protocol II did the same for non-international armed conflicts, including civil wars.

The 1980s and 90s saw other international treaties come into force, banning certain conventional weapons, such as antipersonnel landmines, as well as chemical weapons. Just last year, more than 100 States signed up to an historic treaty against the use of cluster munitions.

Finally, there has been significant progress in terms of investigating and punishing war crimes, thanks to the work of the international tribunals for the former Yugoslavia and Rwanda, and the establishment of the International Criminal Court.

To me, these are all signs that international humanitarian law is fully capable of keeping up with the times.

What else should be done to develop IHL and what are some other current challenges you observe with respect to the law and the realities on the ground?

There is still room to strengthen and clarify the existing legal framework. For example, the ICRC recently published interpretive guidance on the concept of "direct participation in hostilities." Neither the Geneva Conventions nor the Additional Protocols spell out what this actually means. Yet this is crucial because, under the law, civilians lose their protection against attack when and for as long as they directly participate in hostilities. If there is no shared understanding of what this means, there is a risk that civilians will fall victim to erroneous or arbitrary attacks.

Let me give you an example. Imagine a civilian truck driver is delivering ammunition to a shooting position on a front line. This would almost certainly be regarded as taking a direct part in hostilities. But what if that same driver transports ammunition from a factory to a port far away from the conflict zone? In our view, while he is still supporting the war effort, this driver is not directly participating in the fighting and is therefore protected against attack.

These questions are all the more pertinent when you consider that traditional military functions are increasingly being outsourced to private contractors, and that civilians regularly support non-State armed groups through a range of activities, from military and logistical support to feeding and sheltering fighters.

There are other challenges concerning non-international armed conflicts, where some key humanitarian problems are not covered by existing IHL treaties. Customary IHL rules have filled some of these gaps but there are areas where the law could be further clarified and developed. For example, there is currently no detailed framework establishing procedural safeguards for people interned for security reasons in relation to non-international armed conflicts. Such safeguards are necessary to ensure, for example, that people are only held if a valid reason exists.

The so-called "global war on terror" has led to a lot of debate about IHL. What do the Geneva Conventions and the Additional Protocols actually say about the phenomenon of terrorism?

I think it's fair to say that what happened on 11 September 2001 and its aftermath put IHL to one of its toughest tests so far.

Fundamentally, there were differing opinions as to whether the "war on terror" actually amounted to an armed conflict. Similarly, there was discussion as to whether suspected terrorists detained within the context of this fight were covered by IHL.

I personally believe that the Conventions and the Additional Protocols do hold many relevant answers here. After all, terrorism is not a new phenomenon. Both the Fourth Geneva Convention and the Additional Protocols specifically prohibit acts of terrorism.

In terms of addressing threats posed by terrorism, I also believe that the Conventions do a good job of balancing State security concerns and respect for human dignity.

But IHL must only be applied to situations were the fight against terrorism actually amounts to a war. Terrorist acts committed outside of armed conflict must be addressed by means of domestic or international law enforcement, rather than by applying IHL. Such means include intelligence gathering, police and judicial cooperation, the freezing of assets or diplomatic and economic pressure on States accused of aiding suspected terrorists. IHL shouldn't be made to apply to situations for which it was not designed.

Still, the debate sparked off by the events of 11 September has revealed some possible gaps or shortcomings in IHL. For example, concerning the detention of terror suspects in situations of armed conflict, certain aspects of Common Article 3 are vague and need further clarification. For instance, when it comes to conditions of detention, the law should go beyond the basic notion of humane treatment and be more specific. Similarly, no detailed guidance exists on the procedural safeguards (review of grounds for detention) to which people detained for security reasons are entitled.

As you pointed out earlier, the Second World War prompted the ICRC to renew its push for the Conventions to be extended to protect civilians. Why was this significant and how have things changed since then?

Back in 1949, everyone was still reeling from World War II—a global armed conflict of unparalleled proportions. It involved the majority of the world's nations and the mobilization of over 100 million military personnel. More than 70 million people—mostly civilians—were killed, making it the deadliest conflict in human history.

The Fourth Geneva Convention and, later, the Additional Protocols, were major breakthroughs in terms of offering protection to civilians, but the sad reality is that they continue to bear the brunt of war today.

One of the main changes we've seen since 1949 is the increasingly asymmetric nature of warfare. By this, I mean situations where the training and weaponry of one side are far superior to those of the other. Typically, this happens when well-equipped and trained armed forces confront rebel groups. These differences have, in some cases, been used by the weaker side to explain why it has not respected fundamental rules of IHL. This can easily result in a vicious circle where either party justifies its failure to respect IHL by pointing the finger at their enemy.

Another noteworthy development is that military operations have increasingly taken place in densely populated urban areas, often using heavy or highly explosive weapons. From Grozny to Mogadishu and from Baghdad to Gaza City, armed conflict has had a devastating impact on the civilian population.

What do the people most affected by war think about issues like the protection of civilians or acceptable behavior in warfare? Do the people you seek to help believe that the Geneva Conventions are effective?

The ICRC recently commissioned an opinion poll in eight conflict- and violence-affected nations, which asked people about their views on the conduct of hostilities and other related issues.

The vast majority of people support the core principles of IHL and the idea that even wars should have limits, but the research also shows that, in reality, far fewer are aware that the rules exist. Meanwhile, some doubt that the law has a real impact on the ground.

This, coupled with the fact that civilians keep on being killed, separated from their loved ones and forced to flee their homes in conflicts across the globe, indicates that what we really need is better compliance with the law.

In the United States, Arms Sales Policies Changed During the War on Terror

Rachel Stohl

In the following viewpoint, Rachel Stohl argues thatAmerican arms sales policies changed dramatically following the September 11, 2001, terrorist attacks. One of the biggest changes involved lifting arms sales sanctions on countries that had previously committed human rights violations as long as they were considered allies in the War on Terror. Stohl cautions that these transfers of weapons to nations with histories of violations could pose security risks to America in the future. Stohl is a senior analyst for the Center for Defense Information.

As you read, consider the following questions:

1. How did the 9/11 attacks change American arms deal policies?
2. Following the 9/11, which countries did the Bush administration succeed in lifting arms sale sanctions for?
3. How many weapons did the Government Accountability Office report had gone missing in Iraq 2007?

"Questionable Reward: Arms Sales and the War on Terrorism," by Rachel Stohl, Arms Control Today (Jan/Feb 2008). Reprinted by permission.

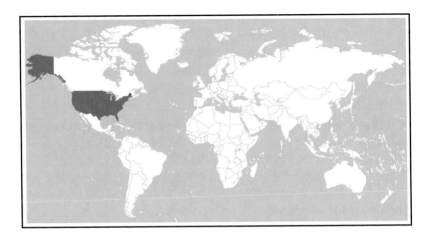

I n November 2007, Pakistan's president, General Pervez Musharraf, invoked emergency rule, suspended the constitution, and arrested thousands of opponents and human rights advocates. As other countries, such as the Netherlands and Switzerland, immediately suspended military aid and weapons deals, the United States, which has given Pakistan more than $10 billion in military assistance since September 11, 2001, decided it would review US arms transfers to Pakistan. Washington also indicated it would likely not prevent any weapons transfers, asserting such a decision could undermine counterterrorism efforts.[1]

US policy toward Pakistan is part of a larger trend of US arms export policy since the September 11 attacks, whereby the United States has made the "global war on terror" its priority in determining arms transfers and military assistance. In the last six years, Washington has stepped up its sales and transfers of high-technology weapons, military training, and other military assistance to governments regardless of their respect for human rights, democratic principles, or nonproliferation. All that matters is that they have pledged their assistance in the global war on terrorism.

US Arms Sales and Export Policy Before and After September 11

To be sure, the United States traditionally has used arms sales to "reward" those countries willing to support its policies. The claimed motivations of such policies have changed over time from anti-communism to democracy building to anti-terrorism. The basic notion of using arms sales as a means of promoting loyalty to US goals has been consistent.

Throughout this period, the United States has dominated the global arms market and continues to do so today. In 2006, Washington concluded the largest number of new arms deals ($16.9 billion worth in 2006, 41.9 percent of the global total) and made the most actual arms deliveries ($14 billion, nearly 52 percent of global arms deliveries).[2] The United States' closest competitors were Russia and the United Kingdom, which made $8.7 billion and $3.1 billion in new deals, respectively, and delivered $5.8 billion and $3.3 billion worth of weapons. The United States has also regained its position atop exporters to the developing world, the largest purchasers of arms. Although the total global value of arms agreements fell in 2006, the United States saw multibillion-dollar increases in the value of its arms transfer agreements worldwide and with the developing world.

Post-September 11 Policy Changes

Nonetheless, there have been important changes since the September 11 attacks, with the United States finessing its arms export policies to support its war on terrorism. The most significant changes have involved the lifting of sanctions, the increase of arms and military training provided to perceived anti-terrorist allies, and the development of new programs focused and based on the global anti-terrorist crusade. To understand and document this trend, the Center for Defense Information has analyzed military assistance data (using US government data solely) for 25 countries[3] that have been identified by the United States as having a strategic role in the war on terrorism. These countries include those that reflect the counterterrorism priorities of the United States—17 are "frontline" states identified by the Bush administration as "countries that cooperate with the United States in the war on terrorism or face terrorist threats themselves"—and others strategically located near Afghanistan and Iraq.

Lifting Sanctions

Immediately after the attacks of September 11, the Bush administration proposed allowing arms sales to potential anti-terrorist allies that had previously been blocked from weapons transfers because they had committed significant human rights violations, lacked sufficient democratic institutions, had been involved in acts of aggression, or had tested nuclear weapons. Congressional opposition prevented these sanctions from being lifted en bloc, and as a result, decisions to lift sanctions were made on a case-by-case basis. To date, the United States has completely lifted pre-September 11 sanctions on Armenia, Azerbaijan, India, Pakistan, Tajikistan, and the former Federal Republic of Yugoslavia (now Montenegro and Serbia). Since September 11, 2001, additional military assistance restrictions to Thailand and Indonesia have been waived.

These countries have been identified as key allies in the global war on terrorism, but each has troubling recent pasts, which led to them being placed on the list in the first place. Not only is each country involved in interstate or intrastate conflicts, but India and Pakistan have been criticized for their evolving nuclear weapons programs, Pakistan's and Thailand's military governments attained power as a result of coups, Azerbaijan has been embroiled for well more than a decade in a shaky cease-fire with Armenia, the stability of Tajikistan remains questionable, and the human rights record of Indonesia's military remains of great concern. Although sanctions have been removed, the conditions in these countries have not improved and in many cases have become worse. Nonetheless, arms transfers and other military assistance to all have increased. In addition, the human rights records of many of these countries have actually worsened, with increasing abuses by government and security forces. US transfers could fuel these human rights abuses and continuing conflict. If the events of September 11, 2001, had never happened, these countries would likely still remain under strict US sanctions.

Increasing Arms and Training to Anti-Terrorism Allies

The second policy shift has been the Bush administration's commitment to using US weapons to arm potential allies in the war against terrorism. On the six-month anniversary of the September 11 attacks, President George W. Bush declared that the United States was willing to provide training and assistance to any government facing a terrorist threat, stating that "America encourages and expects governments everywhere to help remove the terrorist parasites that threaten their own countries and peace of the world. If governments need training, or resources to meet this commitment, America will help."[4]

In addition to the six countries that have had their sanctions lifted, the United States has provided military assistance to some countries that it had not aided previously in this way. For example, Yemen has received grants to acquire U.S weaponry for the last six years, but none in the 11 years prior to 2001. Turkmenistan is now buying US weaponry, and Kyrgyzstan is now permitted to make commercial purchases of US weapons. Even more telling, 18 of the 25 countries in this series received more military assistance and 16 concluded more arms sales with the United States during the five years after the September 11 attacks than they had during the period following the end of the Cold War (fiscal years 1990-2001).

In the first five years following September 11, 2001, the United States sold nearly five times more weapons through Foreign Military Sales (FMS) and Direct Commercial Sales (DCS) to these 25 countries than during the five years prior to that date. From fiscal year 2002 through fiscal year 2006, FMS to these countries increased from about $1.7 billion to $5.3 billion. DCS for these 25 countries have also reached new highs, rising from $72 million during fiscal years 1997–2001 to more than $3 billion during fiscal years 2002-2006. Pakistan had the largest increase in military sales (FMS and DCS) in the five-year period, signing agreements for $3.6 billion in US defense articles. Other beneficiaries of the war on terrorism arms sale bonanza were Bahrain, which saw an increase of $1.6 billion, and Algeria, which saw an increase of nearly $600 million.

In Iraq, we have witnessed some of the drawbacks of this rush to arm and equip countries. In July 2007, the Government Accountability Office (GAO) released a report that revealed that nearly 200,000 weapons and other military equipment that the United States had provided to Iraqi security forces had not been accounted for. Among the weaknesses noted by the GAO was that the Department of Defense, which oversees the Iraqi train-and-equip program, neglected to implement basic accountability procedures to keep track of the distribution of weapons issued in 2004 and 2005.[5] Today, the United States has not enunciated a clear plan to remedy these kinds of problems. Yet, as recently as September 2007, the top US commander in Iraq, General David Petraeus, urged Washington to increase weapons sales to Iraq as soon as possible.

The United States has also viewed military training as an important aspect of its focus on fighting terrorism. A telling statement for the direction of US policy was made in March 2002, when Bush emphasized US reliance on training programs. He said, "We will not send American troops to every battle, but America will actively prepare other nations for the battles ahead."[6] Since September 11, 2001, the United States has offered military training to many countries that have experienced terrorism on their own soil, are struggling with the presence of terrorist networks, or are essential to US counterterrorism strategy.

The overall funding for the International Military Education and Training (IMET) program has grown dramatically since 2001. For the 25 countries, the IMET program grew from $39 million in the five years prior to September 11, 2001, to $93 million in the five years after the attacks. That has also meant that the 25 countries are receiving an even greater percentage of total US military training funds. In 2001 the 25 countries received 15 percent of total IMET funds, but by 2006, their share had jumped to nearly 25 percent.

Although some of these countries are clearly involved with US efforts to defeat al Qaeda and other terrorist networks, with others, such as those in Africa and Asia, the United States is gambling that military training will buy allies in the long run. Military training in many instances promotes the readiness, efficiency, and effectiveness of foreign military troops. It may also worsen the situation in countries plagued by terrorism if a well-armed and unaccountable military is not kept in check with human rights training and the country does not receive assistance building legal and judicial structures. Economic and social aid should also be offered concurrently to help strengthen and promote internal stability. Moreover, in some countries, such as Colombia, Nepal, and the Philippines, what is being described as counterterrorism training is in practice counterinsurgency training. The United States is involving itself in internal conflicts around the world and is in practice encouraging countries to continue their internal struggles that predate September 11, 2001. Not every insurgency is a threat to US security, and some may in fact have very little to do with halting the spread of terrorism worldwide.

The Bush administration argues that professionalizing the world's militaries will help prevent human rights abuses down the road. Yet, the Department of State reveals in its annual human rights report that "serious," "grave," or "significant" abuses were committed by the government or state security forces in more than one-half of the 25 countries profiled in 2006 alone.[7] In many cases, US military assistance to these countries is growing at the same time as human rights conditions are worsening. Ethiopia, which is carrying out a brutal counterinsurgency campaign within its own borders, also launched an invasion of Somalia in December 2006 blamed for the deaths of scores of civilians and the displacement of at least 100,000 Somalis in indiscriminate violence in and around Mogadishu. Chad, which suffers from widespread turmoil and corruption, employs child soldiers in the ranks of its national army and is at a minimum tacitly involved in the ongoing regional conflicts in the Central African Republic and Sudan. By providing military assistance with a disregard for human rights conditions, the United States is not only giving up the opportunity to use military assistance as leverage to improve human rights conditions, but is also rewarding abusive governments for their unconscionable actions.

Moreover, in some of these countries, the military has contributed to domestic political turmoil and instability. In 2006 and 2007, Chad, Nepal, Pakistan, and Thailand dealt with pervasive and significant upheaval. Nepalese security forces opened fire on peaceful strikes and anti-government demonstrations. Chad's government barely survived a coup attempt. Thailand's government was taken over in a "peaceful" military coup. The Musharraf government's continuing battle against reform and political challengers led to the imposition of emergency rule, a move that abandons any pretense of democratic principles.

Establishment of New Programs

The third significant policy shift has been the creation of new Defense Department programs that provide training and weapons for counterterrorism operations outside traditional avenues of support. The Pentagon has long sought the freedom to provide military assistance without human rights conditions or other restrictions under current US law as enunciated in the Foreign Assistance Act. In fiscal year 2002, the Regional Defense Counterterrorism Fellowship Program (CTFP) was created by Congress through the defense appropriations act with a mandate to provide nonlethal anti-terrorism training. In fiscal year 2004, it began offering lethal training. In fiscal year 2006, Congress authorized the Defense Department to use $200 million of its operation and maintenance funds to equip and train foreign militaries for counterterrorism operations, so-called Section 1206 authority.

Creating these parallel training authorities and funding them through the defense budget allows the Pentagon to bypass the Foreign Assistance Act and limits congressional oversight and the normally more cautious State Department from these decisions. In particular, it could help to sidestep restrictions on training or arming human rights abusers. For example, it could be argued that the CTFP essentially serves the same purpose as the State Department's IMET program but without any of the oversight or conditions.

The newly created Defense Department programs have provided training and equipment to all but four of the 25 countries examined. These programs come in addition to the aid provided through the five traditional major military assistance programs. For example, Yemen received more than $4 million in Section 1206 funding in fiscal year 2006 and an additional $200,000 in CTFP funding in fiscal year 2005, as well as $19.6 million in the five traditional types of aid in fiscal year 2006 and $14.6 million in such aid in fiscal year 2005.

Implications of Post-September 11 Policy Changes

Although the dollar value of the increased support for these countries could be seen as relatively insignificant compared to the considerably greater military assistance given to NATO allies or countries in the Middle East, the relative shift from no or very few sales to millions or billions in military assistance in some cases matters greatly. After all, these sales are likely to mark only the beginning of US military and defense industry ties with these questionable and challenging allies. The US defense industry often relies on initial sales in order to encourage future sales; develop maintenance, consulting, or upgrades contracts; and set the stage for larger-ticket items down the road. Using the war on terrorism as their entrance card, these traditionally undesirable partners have gotten their feet in the door and will likely enjoy long-term military relationships with the United States. Indeed, for the most part, sales and training to these countries have grown every year.

The United States must question whether these new allies and these transfers are consistent with long-standing principles and tenets of US law.

Second, these transfers could pose significant risks to long-term US security and stability. From the outset, much of this military assistance is inconsistent with US efforts to spread peace and democracy throughout the world. Beyond the theoretical or principled contradiction, however, the reality is that once these weapons leave US possession and training courses are completed, the United States cannot control how or by whom the weapons are used or the training is implemented. The situation in Iraq demonstrates this reality: US weapons intended for Iraqi security forces have ended up in the hands of insurgents in Iraq and Turkey. In many cases, the countries receiving US military assistance have only pledged assistance to the war on terrorism and may in fact behave in ways the United States opposes. Yet, little can be done in response beyond limiting future weapons and training.

Moreover, the United States suffers from the possibility of blowback—having these weapons used against US troops, civilians, or interests down the road—a phenomenon the United States has experienced firsthand in Afghanistan and Iraq. Weapons provided to the mujahideen in the 1980s were used by the Taliban and today's Afghan rebels. In Iraq, weapons provided to Saddam Hussein during the 1980s remain in circulation and in the hands of Iraqi insurgents. The Bush administration's policy of arming these new allies for short-term gains could put the United States at considerable risk and result in the United States facing its own weapons as political alliances deteriorate. Because the United States has increased transfers and training to countries that have dismal records on democracy, human rights, and loyalty, it is not too far a stretch to believe that some of these new allies could turn against the United States in the future.

The track records of many of these recipients—poor human rights records, prior support for and harboring of terrorists, or consistently undemocratic regimes—have been ignored by the

Bush administration in an effort to bolster the war on terrorism. In doing so, the United States loses the ability to encourage a change in these bad actors' behavior and does not guarantee that these short-term allies will remain long-term US partners. Furthermore, the instability in many of these countries also raises questions about their future allegiance.

Ironically, the provision of weapons, aid, and training to some states might even ultimately serve to undermine the US goal of eradicating terrorism. Countries benefiting from new access to weapons and training may see the continuation of the war on terrorism to be in their own best interest. They may not seriously commit to fighting terrorism because an end to terrorist threats, either real or perceived, might mean a decrease in aid. Thus, the actual dedication of many of these countries to US goals and policies may leave much to be desired.

Conclusion

Rather than continuing its current approach, the United States would be better served by abiding by its long-standing arms export laws to ensure that weapons exports do not undermine security and stability, weaken democracy, support military coups, escalate arms races, exacerbate ongoing conflicts, or cause arms buildups in unstable regions or are used to commit human rights abuses. Although the war on terrorism has taken center stage, these principles and values should not be given an end run. This may mean that even close allies, such as Djibouti, Ethiopia, and Pakistan, which have worsening or no improvement in their human rights records, have their military assistance scaled back until substantial improvements are made. The United States should look at other ways of cooperating with new allies, such as economic and development assistance, and work to strengthen these partners' democracies and institutions. More than ever, the United States needs strong partners that value human rights and the rule of law.

If arms and training are the only foreign policy tools the United States is willing to use, then they must be provided in line with US law and under the strictest oversight and accountability. Programs should not be allowed to bypass US law. New Defense Department programs should be scaled back and evaluated, rather than expanded, to ensure that they are upholding US law. If the United States does sell weapons and provide training to questionable new allies, all effort should be taken to ensure that these weapons do not undermine US security down the road.

Endnotes

1. Wade Boese, "US Pakistani Arms Pipeline Stays Open," Arms Control Today, December 2007, p. 29. Emergency rule lasted from Nov. 3 to Dec. 15, during which time Musharraf resigned from the military but retained his presidency.
2. Richard F. Grimmett, "Conventional Arms Transfers to Developing Nations, 1999-2006," CRS Report for Congress, RL34187, September 26, 2007.
3. Algeria, Armenia, Azerbaijan, Bahrain, Chad, Djibouti, Ethiopia, Georgia, India, Indonesia, Kazakhstan, Kenya, Kyrgyzstan, Mali, Mauritania, Nepal, Niger, Oman, Pakistan, Philippines, Tajikistan, Thailand, Turkmenistan, Uzbekistan, and Yemen.
4. Office of the Press Secretary, The White House, "President Thanks World Coalition for Anti-Terrorism Efforts," Washington, DC, March 11, 2002 (hereinafter president's remarks, March 11, 2002).
5. US Government Accountability Office, "Stabilizing Iraq: DOD Cannot Ensure That US-Funded Equipment Has Reached Iraqi Security Forces," July 31, 2007.
6. President's remarks, March 11, 2002.
7. US Department of State, "2006 Country Reports on Human Rights Practices." Posted: January 25, 2008.

In the Middle East, CIA Intervention Does More Harm than Good

Garikai Chengu

In the following viewpoint, Garikai Chengu argues that American foreign policy has helped terrorist organizations like al-Qaeda and ISIS form. In the 1970s, the CIA provided weapons and training to Islamic extremists engaged in conflict against the Soviet Union. The CIA provided training to Osama bin Laden, who in 2001 would orchestrate one of the deadliest terrorist attacks on American soil. Following the attacks, the Bush administration started the War on Terror, which sparked the formation of the al-Qaeda splinter group ISIS. Chengu is a research scholar at Harvard University.

As you read, consider the following questions:

1. Where did the name al-Qaeda come from?
2. How did American policy in Iraq worsen existing divisions within the country?
3. As of the publishing of this article how much money had the United States spent on the War on Terror?

Much like Al Qaeda, the Islamic State (ISIS) is made-in-the-USA, an instrument of terror designed to divide and conquer the oil-rich Middle East and to counter Iran's growing influence in the region.

"How the US Helped Create Al Qaeda and ISIS," by Garikai Chengu, CounterPunch, September 19, 2014. Reprinted by permission.

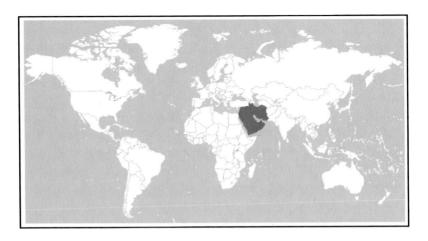

The fact that the United States has a long and torrid history of backing terrorist groups will surprise only those who watch the news and ignore history.

The CIA first aligned itself with extremist Islam during the Cold War era. Back then, America saw the world in rather simple terms: on one side, the Soviet Union and Third World nationalism, which America regarded as a Soviet tool; on the other side, Western nations and militant political Islam, which America considered an ally in the struggle against the Soviet Union.

The director of the National Security Agency under Ronald Reagan, General William Odom recently remarked, "by any measure the US has long used terrorism. In 1978–79 the Senate was trying to pass a law against international terrorism—in every version they produced, the lawyers said the US would be in violation."

During the 1970ss the CIA used the Muslim Brotherhood in Egypt as a barrier, both to thwart Soviet expansion and prevent the spread of Marxist ideology among the Arab masses. The United States also openly supported Sarekat Islam against Sukarno in Indonesia, and supported the Jamaat-e-Islami terror group against Zulfiqar Ali Bhutto in Pakistan. Last but certainly not least, there is Al Qaeda.

Lest we forget, the CIA gave birth to Osama Bin Laden and breastfed his organization during the 1980's. Former British Foreign Secretary, Robin Cook, told the House of Commons that Al Qaeda was unquestionably a product of Western intelligence agencies. Mr. Cook explained that Al Qaeda, which literally means an abbreviation of "the database" in Arabic, was originally the computer database of the thousands of Islamist extremists, who were trained by the CIA and funded by the Saudis, in order to defeat the Russians in Afghanistan.

America's relationship with Al Qaeda has always been a love-hate affair. Depending on whether a particular Al Qaeda terrorist group in a given region furthers American interests or not, the US State Department either funds or aggressively targets that terrorist group. Even as American foreign policy makers claim to oppose Muslim extremism, they knowingly foment it as a weapon of foreign policy.

The Islamic State is its latest weapon that, much like Al Qaeda, is certainly backfiring. ISIS recently rose to international prominence after its thugs began beheading American journalists. Now the terrorist group controls an area the size of the United Kingdom.

In order to understand why the Islamic State has grown and flourished so quickly, one has to take a look at the organization's American-backed roots. The 2003 American invasion and occupation of Iraq created the pre-conditions for radical Sunni groups, like ISIS, to take root. America, rather unwisely, destroyed Saddam Hussein's secular state machinery and replaced it with a predominantly Shiite administration. The US occupation caused vast unemployment in Sunni areas, by rejecting socialism and closing down factories in the naive hope that the magical hand of the free market would create jobs. Under the new US-backed Shiite regime, working class Sunni's lost hundreds of thousands of jobs. Unlike the white Afrikaners in South Africa, who were allowed to keep their wealth after regime change, upper class Sunni's were systematically dispossessed of their assets and lost their political influence. Rather than promoting religious integration and unity, American policy in Iraq exacerbated sectarian divisions and created a fertile breeding ground for Sunni discontent, from which Al Qaeda in Iraq took root.

The Islamic State of Iraq and Syria (ISIS) used to have a different name: Al Qaeda in Iraq. After 2010 the group rebranded and refocused its efforts on Syria.

There are essentially three wars being waged in Syria: one between the government and the rebels, another between Iran and Saudi Arabia, and yet another between America and Russia. It is this third, neo-Cold War battle that made US foreign policy makers decide to take the risk of arming Islamist rebels in Syria, because Syrian President, Bashar al-Assad, is a key Russian ally. Rather embarrassingly, many of these Syrian rebels have now turned out to be ISIS thugs, who are openly brandishing American-made M16 Assault rifles.

America's Middle East policy revolves around oil and Israel. The invasion of Iraq has partially satisfied Washington's thirst for oil, but ongoing air strikes in Syria and economic sanctions on Iran have everything to do with Israel. The goal is to deprive Israel's neighboring enemies, Lebanon's Hezbollah and Palestine's Hamas, of crucial Syrian and Iranian support.

ISIS is not merely an instrument of terror used by America to topple the Syrian government; it is also used to put pressure on Iran.

The last time Iran invaded another nation was in 1738. Since independence in 1776, the US has been engaged in over 53 military invasions and expeditions. Despite what the Western media's war cries would have you believe, Iran is clearly not the threat to regional security, Washington is. An Intelligence Report published in 2012, endorsed by all sixteen US intelligence agencies, confirms that Iran ended its nuclear weapons program in 2003. Truth is, any Iranian nuclear ambition, real or imagined, is as a result of American hostility towards Iran, and not the other way around.

America is using ISIS in three ways: to attack its enemies in the Middle East, to serve as a pretext for US military intervention abroad, and at home to foment a manufactured domestic threat, used to justify the unprecedented expansion of invasive domestic surveillance.

By rapidly increasing both government secrecy and surveillance, Mr. Obama's government is increasing its power to watch its citizens, while diminishing its citizens' power to watch their government. Terrorism is an excuse to justify mass surveillance, in preparation for mass revolt.

The so-called "War on Terror" should be seen for what it really is: a pretext for maintaining a dangerously oversized US military. The two most powerful groups in the US foreign policy establishment are the Israel lobby, which directs US Middle East policy, and the Military-Industrial-Complex, which profits from the former group's actions. Since George W. Bush declared the "War on Terror" in October 2001, it has cost the American taxpayer approximately 6.6 trillion dollars and thousands of fallen sons and daughters; but, the wars have also raked in billions of dollars for Washington's military elite.

In fact, more than seventy American companies and individuals have won up to $27 billion in contracts for work in postwar Iraq and Afghanistan over the last three years, according to a recent study by the Center for Public Integrity. According to the study, nearly 75 per cent of these private companies had employees or board members, who either served in, or had close ties to, the executive branch of the Republican and Democratic administrations, members of Congress, or the highest levels of the military.

In 1997, a US Department of Defense report stated, "the data show a strong correlation between US involvement abroad and an increase in terrorist attacks against the US" Truth is, the only way America can win the "War On Terror" is if it stops giving terrorists the motivation and the resources to attack America. Terrorism is the symptom; American imperialism in the Middle East is the cancer. Put simply, the War on Terror is terrorism; only, it is conducted on a much larger scale by people with jets and missiles.

Periodical and Internet Sources Bibliography

The following articles have been selected to supplement the diverse views presented in this chapter.

David Alpher, "ISIS Attacks Fueled by Illegal Guns and Open Societies We Can't Afford to Lose," The Conversation, Nov 19, 2015, https://theconversation.com/isis-attacks-fueled-by-illegal-guns-and-open-societies-we-cant-afford-to-lose-50735.

Emma Anderson, "How German Guns Often End Up in Child Soldiers' Hands," The Local, Feb 10, 2017 https://www.thelocal.de/20170210/study-shows-how-german-guns-are-landing-in-child-soldiers-hands.

Brian DeLay, "How the US Government Created and Coddled the Gun Industry," The Conversation, Oct 9, 2017, https://theconversation.com/how-the-us-government-created-and-coddled-the-gun-industry-85167.

Steve Jones, "The Geneva Accords 1954," Thoughtco, May 17, 2017, https://www.thoughtco.com/the-geneva-accords-1954-3310118.

Anup Shah, "Arms Trade—A Major Cause of Suffering," Global Issues, June 30, 2013, http://www.globalissues.org/issue/73/arms-trade-a-major-cause-of-suffering.

Anup Shah, "Small Arms—They Cause 90% of Civilian Casualties," Global Issues, Jan 21, 2006, http://www.globalissues.org/article/78/small-arms-they-cause-90-of-civilian-casualties.

UN, "Strong Link Between Child Soldiers and Small Arms Trade," UN experts say, UN, July 15, 2008, https://www.un.org/apps/news/story.asp?NewsID=27382.

UN Security Council, "Human Cost of Illicit Flow of Small Arms, Light Weapons Stressed in Security Council Debate," UN, 13 MAY 2015, https://www.un.org/press/en/2015/sc11889.doc.htm.

| Nuclear Proliferation

In the United States and the Soviet Union, the Theory of Mutually Assured Destruction Altered International Relations

Fait Muedini

In the following viewpoint, Fait Muedini examines the effect of Mutually Assured Destruction (MAD) theory on international relations. In essence, the theory was that countries would be less likely to use nuclear weapons on countries who could fire them back. Historians believe the MAD theory helped spark an arms race between the two nations and helped form several proxy wars. The likelihood that nuclear weapons will be used relies less on their existence and more on the beliefs of those who have the power to wield them. Muedini is the Frances Shera Fessler Professor of International Studies at Butler University.

As you read, consider the following questions:

1. What is the MAD theory?
2. What year did the Soviet Union acquire nuclear weapons?
3. How did the MAD theory contribute to the arms race?

Mutually Assured Destruction theory (MAD) was a very important idea in the history of international relations, particularly with regards to discussions of state security,

"Mutually Assured Destruction," International Relations, May 17, 2016. Reprinted by permission.

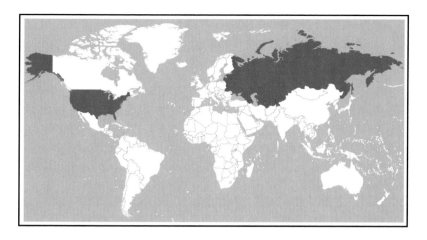

international security, as it related to nuclear weapons, and particularly from the 1960s until the 1980s. In this article, we shall define and discuss mutually assured destruction theory in international relations. We will trade the history of the theory, how mutually assured destruction was viewed by the United States and the Soviet Union during the Cold War, arguments of those who supported MAD, and also criticisms of the theory. We will then end the article with a discussion on how mutually assured destruction is viewed today in contemporary international relations theory.

What Is Mutually Assured Destruction?

In international relations, mutually assured destruction theory is the idea that if two more states in the international system have nuclear weapons capabilities, then this will be enough to deter any one state from carrying out a nuclear attack. The reason is that if the first state were to launch a nuclear strike, the second state (and any other states who have nuclear weapons) could retaliate, which in turn would lead to additional attacks by the first state. This would result in mutually assured destruction of the states involved. Because of this, the theory suggests that no state would be willing to initiate a nuclear strike for fear of the consequences that that initial strike would bring.

History of Mutually Assured Destruction

The topic of mutually assured destruction was highly discussed in the middle to later years of the 20th century. Coming out of World War II, two major superpowers existed: the United States and the Soviet Union. Not only did these states rival one another in terms of military power, but they also had conflicting political ideologies, with the US focused on ideas of capitalism, as well as civil and political-based rights systems, whereas the Soviet Union emphasized socialist and communist systems, along with socio-economic based rights. Throughout the late 1940s, the 1950s, and onwards, these two states were engaged in a war of ideologies, which then turned into a series of proxy wars throughout the globe. All this time, the two sides provided billions of dollars of military weaponry, as well as money, for their political and ideological allies.

What made the situation far more of a concern was the role of nuclear weapons. The United States was the only state in the history of the world to use nuclear weapons in combat, carrying out two nuclear bombs on Hiroshima and Nagasaki, Japan during World War II. From 1945, until 1949, the United States was the only power in the world with nuclear capabilities. However, all of this changed in 1949, when the Soviet Union was able to develop their own nuclear weapons.

However, the idea of Mutually Assured Destruction as a United States Foreign Policy did not arise until the 1960s. More specifically, it was a speech given by Robert McNamara, who was the United States Secretary of Defense to President John F. Kennedy. It was in 1962 that McNamara, in a speech to the American Bar Foundation, outlined his position on mutual assured destruction, and in particular, through a buildup of nuclear weapons (de Castella, 2012). McNamara's position was that in the event that the Soviet Union would set a nuclear strike against the United States, the US in turn could unleash a large nuclear counterstrike, one so large that it would lead to an "assured destruction" of the USSR (de Castella, 2012). And because of this counter threat the US posed, the Soviet Union would not begin a nuclear war.

Again, for many in the US leadership in the early 1960s, mutually assured destruction was to be used only in the case of an attack. However, it is important to note that there were other approaches to dealing with the Soviet Union in the late 1940s and 1950s that actually included the possibility of using nuclear weapons; some were willing to consider this possibility.

Scholars of nuclear weapons and the Cold War point out that in the late 1940s, and more-so in the 1960s, there was a belief among many that a nuclear war would not break out because each side had nuclear weapons. This is where we saw the arguments of mutually assured destruction initiate from. Two countries, knowing the power of one another, would not risk an all-out nuclear war that would be sure to decimate each country, if not the entire world. At least, that was the belief.

However, the Cuban Missile Crisis of 1962 increased the concern about the possibility of a nuclear war between the USSR and the United States.

But with the nuclear crisis avoided, tensions continued between the two states. While there was the years "detente in the 1970s, tension rose again in the 1980s. By this point the Soviet Union had many more warheads, and it was commonly said that there were enough nuclear arms on Earth to wipe the planet out several times" (de Castella, 2012). In addition, "In 1983 there were a number of Russian false alarms. The Soviet Union's early warning system mistakenly picked up a US missile coming into USSR airspace. In the same year, NATO's military planning operation Able Archer led some Russian commanders to conclude that a NATO nuclear launch was imminent" (de Castella, 2012).

The question that drove much of US and Soviet foreign policy primarily revolved around on what effects we would see with two superpowers each having nuclear weapons? This was the reality that both sides were dealing with.

Thus, it is necessary to look at the arguments for and against nuclear weapons and the belief in mutually assured destruction.

Arguments for Mutually Assured Destruction as a Nuclear Deterrent

Staving off of any potential nuclear war: Advocates of Mutually Assured Destruction continue to reference the lack of nuclear war between the US and the USSR as proof that the theory works. For them, it was quite possible that both countries could have fought one another on a number of occasions. But they didn't, with the reason being that both sides knew the consequences of a nuclear conflict. If one was to begin a launch, the other had the nuclear power to strike back forcefully, this could devastate that first country. But if they could survive the retaliatory strike, then they could set off many of their own nuclear weapons, which could in turn cause significant harm to the other state. Thus, to those advocates of this theory, it was specifically because each side had nuclear weapons that conflict was averted.

The reduced need for additional nuclear weapons

One of the other beliefs held by proponents of Mutually Assured Destruction theory argued that MAD would also lead to a reduction in the necessity to develop many nuclear weapons. As Rowen (2004) explains, "MAD was based on the observation that, since only a few nuclear weapons delivered on a city could produce vast damage, why buy more than the number needed to assure that result?" (4). And for those that felt this way, they also saw an increase in nuclear buildup "at best a waste—and at worst destabilizing—to make qualitative improvements, such as installing multiple, independent, reentry vehicles (MIRVs) that would enable a single missile to destroy many enemy silos. Increased missile accuracy was deplored. Also deplorable from this perspective was to try to defend against oncoming missiles" (but what is important to note is that the Soviet Union leaders felt differently than did the leaders in the US government) (Rowen, 2004: 4).

So, with increased nuclear weapons, another country would not dare risk provoking an attack, or receiving a retaliatory response.

This was what many believed, and thus supported nuclear weapons as a deterrent.

It was for this reason that the Mutually Assured Destruction led to what was referred to as an "arms race" between the United States and the Soviet Union? The reason? Some felt that if one of the two superpowers had a clear arms advantage over the others, then the likelihood of a nuclear war breaking out would increase. Therefore, in an attempt to check that possibility, the other side would increase their nuclear arms (Rowen, 2004).

Criticisms of Mutually Assured Destruction

Critics have levied a series of challenges to arguments made by proponents of mutually assured destruction as a viable reason for nuclear war to not break out. Below are the points critics of MAD theory as an effective deterrent have made:

The issue of where a nuclear strike would occur

While those who argue that nuclear weapons are a deterrent to war suggest that if one state launched a strike on another state, that state in turn would respond with its own nuclear attack. However, where this idea becomes complicated is if the first state does not launch at the second (nuclear state), but rather, carries out a nuclear attack against an ally, or a non-aligned state. Would that state be willing to actually use their own nuclear weapons to defend an ally, or another state? There might be some issues salient enough for the government to be responded with in such fashion. But they might not feel it as necessary to defend other areas with the use of nuclear weapons.

The threat to use nuclear weapons for a vulnerable ally

Another related problem with regards to accessibility to nuclear weapons and the threat of their use is with regards to how a superpower might act in attempts to stave off an attack on an area that is unable to defend itself. For example, as Rowen (2004) writes, "A widely held belief from 1949 on was that nuclear war could not happen, especially as both sides acquired large and protected forces. However, there were several arguments why it could, nevertheless, occur. One was the temptation to threaten use of nuclear weapons in support of a vulnerable position, most prominently ours in Western Europe. How could it be rational to adopt a strategy that if carried out would have resulted in vast devastation—including to its purported beneficiary, Europe? The idea was that Soviet leaders would recognize the dangers of invading Europe, perhaps less for concern of a carefully decided American nuclear response than that an unplanned event, perhaps in the fog of war, could somehow lead to nuclear weapons being launched." (2-3).

What is interesting to note is that before the Mutually Assured Destruction position the United States government held in the 1960s, they were very open to being the first to carry out a nuclear strike. This seems counter to the idea that some were holding onto that nuclear war could not happen during this time (in Rowen, 2004).

The willingness of leaders to use nuclear weapons

One of the other more often cited arguments by proponents of nuclear weapons has been the idea that government and military leaders–understanding the grave nature of nuclear attacks–would never want to use them, knowing that a counter-attack would lead to mutually assured destruction of at least two countries, if not the world as a whole. However, there are a few counterpositions to this claim. For one, while this might prevent a leader from wanting to use nuclear weapons, it in no way reduces their belief that another leader would also be unwilling to use nuclear weapons. In addition, there are many examples to suggest that leaders during the Cold War (for example) were considering the use of the nuclear weapons. For example, "A leading scholar of the taboo, Nina Tannenwald, argues that it had become institutionalized within the US government by the beginning of the 1960s and was reoected in the policies of the Kennedy administration. Tannenwald argues that President Kennedy and Secretary of Defense Robert McNamara found the idea of using nuclear weapons largely "unthinkable."" However, in late unclassified documents, McNamara spoke about nuclear weapons as an option if China carried out an addition invasion of India (in Lieber & Press, 2006). In addition, there were called to improve nuclear capabilities in 1961 in case of a US first strike against the Soviet Union (Lieber & Press, 2006).

And even if there is a "taboo" against using nuclear weapons, this might not be the case in high stake issues (Lieber & Press, 2006), leading further concern that mutually assured destruction is really a successful enough deterrent to nuclear war.

The number of individuals who could theoretically launch a nuclear weapon

In popular culture, there is the belief that there are two specific keys that can launch nuclear weapons, and that only two individuals have such keys, and that they must be activated simultaneously in order for a weapon to go off. The idea is that only the very top figures of a government have the ability to launch nuclear weapons, and even more assuring, is that notion that it would take more than one person to do so. The safeguards against an emotionally charged nuclear attack have been avoided. The problem with this that we know of at least one case in which these safeguards were not in place.

Take the issue of the Cuban Missile Crisis between the United States and the Soviet Union. While one might think that the only individuals who had the authorization to launch a nuclear weapon were United States President John F. Kennedy and Soviet Union Premier Nikita Khrushchev. However, what we know is "that the Russian general in charge of the missiles sent to Cuba in 1962 had the authority—and apparently the means—to launch them" (Rowen, 2004). So, while it is true that the United States and the Soviet Union tried to streamline just how a weapon could be launched, the idea that others lower than the top positions could not launch an attack are inaccurate.

In fact, "According to a review of the memoir *My Journey at the Nuclear Brink* by former US Secretary of Defense William J.

Perry on The New York Review of Books, a Soviet submarine stopped at the blockade was armed with nuclear torpedoes and had decided to use them" (Bender, 2016). The commanders of the submarine were given the approval to launch a nuclear strike against the United States. However, it was only because of the top commander, Vasili Arkhipov ordered against this that the nuclear strike did not occur" (Bender, 2016). But had he not made that decision, it is certainly possible that a nuclear war could have been begun.

Reduced Nuclear Capacity

Some scholars have suggested that more important than devoting most of a state's resources to nuclear weapons, a state could build up its conventional military. Those who advocate this position have referred to it as "a "finite deterrent." One only needs to maintain enough nuclear weapons to destroy a large fraction of the opponent's population. A key assumption underlying this school of thought is that nuclear weapons are only effective at deterring one's adversary from making a direct attack on one's homeland. Nuclear weapon's are not capable of deterring attacks against one's allies in other areas of the world" (Hardin & Mearsheimer, 1985: 420). But while this minimizes the reliance on the size of a military's overall nuclear weapons, it still does not rule out using nuclear weapons against a population. This leads to an additional critique of mutual assured destruction, which is related to how to justly go about conflict.

Just War Theory

One additional and highly important factor as to why mutually assured destruction is a bad foreign policy has to do with the moral implications of a nuclear war. An initial nuclear strike, followed by a nuclear retaliatory strike (or strikes) would cost the lives of those living in the the countries being attacked. And for this reason, "Just war theorists are invariably disturbed by the policy of mutually assured destruction since it is predicated on the threat to kill massive number of innocent civilians" (418-419).

And because of this, some have suggested a move to more accurate weapons such as cruise missiles. The issue here is that these could also be turned towards population centers. Another counterargument by MAD supporters is that this approach might make a country vulnerable to an initial nuclear strike (Hardin & Mearsheimer, 1985: 419). There is also a belief that once nuclear weapons exist, being careful with them so that civilians are not hit is not possible (Hardin & Mearsheimer, 1985: 419). For these reasons, there has been a move to eliminate all nuclear weapons in the world.

Is Mutually Assured Destruction Relevant Today?

Part of the reason that mutually assured destruction was so strongly advocated by some proponents of the theory was due to their belief that both the United States as well as the Soviet Union could withstand any first attack by the other sides. And while that might have been the case in the 1960s-1980s, scholars have argued that following the end of the Cold War, the balance of nuclear capabilities has clearly went to the favor of the United States. Writing in 2006, Lieber & Press note that

> the strategic nuclear balance has shifted profoundly. Part of the shift is attributable to the decline of the Russian arsenal. Compared with the Soviet force in 1990, Russia has 58 percent fewer intercontinental ballistic missiles (ICBMs), 39 percent fewer bombers, and 80 percent fewer ballistic missile submarines (SSBNs).16 Furthermore, serious maintenance and readiness problems plague Russia's nuclear forces. Most of Russia's ICBMs have exceeded their service lives, and a series of naval accidents—highlighted by the sinking of the attack submarine Kursk in 2000— reflect the severe decay of the feet.17 Budgetary constraints have also dramatically reduced the frequency of Russia's submarine and mobile ICBM patrols, increasing the vulnerability of what would otherwise be the most survivable element of its arsenal. Since 2000, Russian SSBNs have conducted approximately two patrols per year (with none in 2002), down from sixty in 1990, and apparently Russia often has no

mobile missiles on patrol.18 Finally, Russia has had difficulty maintaining satellite observation of US ICBM fields, and gaps in its radar network would leave it blind to a US submarine-launched ballistic missile (SLBM) attack from launch areas in the Pacific Ocean.(12)

So, while Russia still has thousands of nuclear weapons, their ability to maintain them, as well as their nuclear program is nowhere near what it was during the Cold War period. Couple this with the fact that the United States has continued to improve their military program (through bombers, more precise missiles, etc…) throughout the post-Cold War years, and the imbalance between the two states is quite telling. Given this imbalance, the question that scholars have examined is: in this new post-Cold War period, if the United States was to hypothetically carry out a nuclear strike against a country (such as Russia) (the authors make it clear that they choose Russia as an example only because it is the most difficult case to prove) (Lieber & Press, 2006), could Russia effectively carry out a nuclear counterstrike, thereby showing that mutual assured destruction is still quite possible today? There is a belief that the United States could surprise the USSR with a strike that could halt any sort of counter-attack (Lieber & Press, 2006).

But this idea itself is still risky. With tensions continuing to be high between countries like India and Pakistan, as well as the The United States and Russia, along with North Korea's nuclear tests, there are fears that nuclear weapons are the greatest threat to the survival of all existence. And it is why there continues to be a movement to not only stop the proliferation of new nuclear weapons in the international system, but also to get rid of all nuclear weapons.

References

Bender, J. (2016). The moment when the Soviets decided to use nuclear weapons against the US. Business Insider Malaysia. June 24th, 2016. Available Online: http://www.businessinsider.my/soviets-decided-to-use-nuclear-weapons-2016-6/#BfG5yXQDQUOCfAmY.97.

Brown, J. (2016). A Start Nuclear Warning. New York Review of Books. June 14, 2016. Available Online: http://www.nybooks.com/articles/2016/07/14/a-stark-nuclear-warning/.

De Castella, T. (2012). How did we forget about mutually assured destruction? BBC, 15 February 2012. Available Online: http://www.bbc.com/news/magazine-17026538.

Hardin, R. & Mearsheimer, J. (1985). Introduction. Ethics, Vol. 95, No. 3, pages 411-423. Available Online: http://mearsheimer.uchicago.edu/pdfs/B0001.pdf.

Jervis, R. (2009). The Dustbin of History: Mutual Assured Destruction. Foreign Policy. November 9, 2009. Available Online: http://foreignpolicy.com/2009/11/09/the-dustbin-of-history-mutual-assured-destruction/.

Lieber, K.A. & Press, D.G. (2006). The End of MAD? The Nuclear Dimension of US Primacy. International Security, Vol. 30, No. 4, pages 7-44.

Rowen, H.S. (2004). Introduction. In Getting MAD: Nuclear Mutual Assured Destruction, Its Origins and Practice. Edited by Henry D. Sokolski. Strategic Studies Institute. Available Online: http://www.strategicstudiesinstitute.army.mil/pdffiles/pub585.pdf.

Is the Non-Proliferation Treaty Successful?

Saira Bano

In the following viewpoint, Saira Bano argues that the Non-Proliferation Treaty (NPT) has been successful in many ways, and that we should learn from its successes as much as from its failures. Since its creation in 1970, the NPT has significantly slowed the global development of nuclear weapons. In the past, nations have been offered incentives to either destroy their arsenal or to simply not develop one, but there are few ways to discipline countries that break the NPT. This leaves many to feel the NPT is fragile and ineffective. Bano is a PhD candidate at the Centre for Military and Strategic Studies at the University of Calgary.

As you read, consider the following questions:

1. How many counties have produced nuclear weapons since the creation of the NPT?
2. Why is the NPT considered discriminatory by some?
3. What were some of the incentives used to keep nations from developing nuclear weapons?

The Non-Proliferation Treaty (NPT), despite being discriminatory and fragile, has sustained its existence and currently enjoys near-universal membership. In March 1970, the NPT came into effect and since then has provided a

"Is the NPT Irrelevant?" by Saira Bano, *International Policy Digest*, November 29, 2014. Reprinted by permission.

foundation for legal and political efforts to curb the spread of nuclear weapons. The NPT is a nearly universal (except for India, Pakistan, Israel and North Korea) treaty and the linchpin of the global nonproliferation regime.

The NPT is a bargain between NWSs (nuclear weapons states) and NNWSs (non-nuclear weapons states) in which NWSs (the United States, Russia, France, UK and China) agreed to share nuclear technology for peaceful purposes and gradually disarm their nuclear arsenals while NNWSs agreed not to develop nuclear weapons and to accept IAEA (International Atomic Energy Agency) safeguards. It is pertinent to ask why the NPT, despite its imposition of unequal rights, has survived so long and why the membership has grown to be nearly universal.

In 1963 President Kennedy warned that 15 to 25 nations could possess nuclear weapons within a decade. Forty-four years later, mostly due to the NPT, only nine countries have reached the nuclear-weapon threshold. Forty-four countries are considered to be capable of producing nuclear weapons, but have decided not to develop them. The states that tried to develop them reversed the status of their nuclear arsenals.

In this regard, the treaty is a success. The NPT has provided a mechanism to monitor the nuclear related activities. The treaty and the IAEA safeguards have provided the tools to limit the spread of nuclear weapons. Most of the literature has focused on the failures of the treaty but it is important that the successes should equally be focused on to understand the reasons of these successes and how best these lessons can be implemented to prevent further proliferation.

For most scholars, there has long been a broad consensus that the NPT either has failed or is on the verge of failure. It is long been argued that the treaty will inevitably collapse resulting in a proliferation cascade. The consistency in these pessimistic predictions is remarkable. Such predictions were most frequent in the aftermath of each proliferation crises. India's nuclear test in 1974, the Iraq revelations of a clandestine nuclear program in the early 1990s, the 1998 South Asian nuclear tests, the discovery of the A. Q. Khan network, the North Korean withdrawal from the treaty and most recently the controversy regarding Iran's nuclear program, have generated a large scale analysis about the demise of the treaty and/or a wave of new weapons states.

If the NPT has no direct causal effects on its members to abstain from the nuclear option, the question arises why the pace of nuclear proliferation over the last four decades has been relatively slow. The explanation for non-proliferation must be found outside the treaty framework. There is little doubt that the NPT regime worked well during the Cold War period not because the regime itself exerted some direct effects on its members but rather because the two superpowers had a convergence of interest in creating and maintaining the treaty. There was a common understanding that the world with more nuclear weapons would be much more difficult and dangerous. The history of the NPT points to the fact that many states joined the NPT because of the persuasive powers of the Americans and the Soviets.

The NWSs joined the NPT because it has not only legitimized their nuclear weapons program but also has provided them an effective means to maintain their nuclear dominance. The question arises why the NNWSs joined this discriminatory treaty. There are three types of states that joined the NPT as NNWSs. Small states that lacked the financial and technical capacity to obtain nuclear weapons and therefore, strongly supported the treaty. Medium states with existential threats joined the NPT because of their reliance on the nuclear protection of others. The moral or legal obligations of the treaty were not important rather nuclear protection gave them a cheaper option for their security. Medium states with an existential threat without nuclear protection join the NPT because of their relations with the United States and economic and political interests.

More states have opted to give up their nuclear pursuit than have maintained their arsenals. Both realpolitik and moral factors were important in the abolishment of their nuclear programs.

After the Cold War, financial assistance was offered to Belarus and Ukraine in exchange for the abolishment of their nuclear stockpiles; technical assistance played an importance role in the case of Brazil; and regime change in South Africa explains its denuclearization. Libya was offered an end to its international isolation and the normative component of the non-proliferation norm and economic interests triumphed in the case of Sweden and Switzerland.

The treaty provides legal justification for coercive sanctions when a state tries to acquire nuclear weapons under the cover of the NPT. The violation of the treaty results in coercive economic and military sanctions and isolation. The NPT requires the NWSs to negotiate in good faith to disarm their nuclear arms. The lack of success on this pledge has prompted the NNWSs to reframe their demand for nuclear disarmament with references to the humanitarian consequences of the use of nuclear weapons, international law, and international humanitarian law. This keeps pressure on the NWSs to negotiate and conclude arms control agreement.

The NPT is still considered a legitimate treaty by the majority of states. Even Iran strategically adopts the discourse of the NPT to better pursue its interest. Iran justifies its uranium enrichment program consistent with Article IV of the NPT, which allows developing nuclear technologies for peaceful purposes. Even while breaking the rules, Iran defends its actions as being within the limits of what is permitted in the NPT. This reflects the understanding that the NPT and its rules have become the norm through which Iran protects its interest and the international community justifies its actions against Iran.

The continued long-term viability of the treaty can only be assured through political determination. The treaty is considered as legitimate but the reluctance of the NWSs to disarm their nuclear weapons has created a legitimacy crisis. Nuclear states must address the legitimacy crisis by concluding nuclear arms agreements, such as the CTBT (Comprehensive Test Ban Treaty) and FMCT (Fissile Material Control Treaty) that complement the NPT. During the Cold War the success of the NPT can be attributed to the cooperation of major powers but in the post-Cold War era the major actors have a divergence of interests. For major actors like Russia and China a multipolar nuclear world would upset US dominance.

Without the cooperation of major states it is unlikely that the NPT will be an effective barrier against nuclear proliferation. The NWSs must take a leadership role to address the conflicts in the Middle East, in South East Asia, and on the Korean Peninsula, and they must also take practical steps for eventual disarmament of their nuclear weapons. It is important not to risk the viability of the treaty, which for the past forty-four years has provided an enduring framework to curb nuclear proliferation and has saved the world from the horrors of nuclear use.

Russia, the United States, and Pakistan Have All Come Close to Using Nuclear Weapons by Accident

Gunnar Westberg

In the following viewpoint, Gunnar Westberg details several times when countries came close to launching nuclear weapons based on faulty information or computer glitches. These incidents show how the theory of mutually assured destruction might not prevent the accidental use of such weapons. Westberg shows how permissive links and no-first-use policies can help prevent such deadly mistakes from occurring. Westberg is a professor of medicine and a board member of the Transnational Institute.

As you read, consider the following questions:

1. Who is Colonel Stanislav Petrov?
2. What is a permissive link?
3. What is the nuclear threshold?

T he proposition that nuclear weapons can be retained in perpetuity and never used—accidentally or by decision—defies credibility."

This unanimous statement was published by the Canberra Commission in 1996. Among the commission members were internationally known former ministers of defense and of foreign affairs and generals.

"Close Calls: We Were Much Closer to Nuclear Annihilation Than We Ever Knew," by Gunnar Westberg, International Physicians for the Prevention of Nuclear War, May 23, 2016. Reprinted by permission.

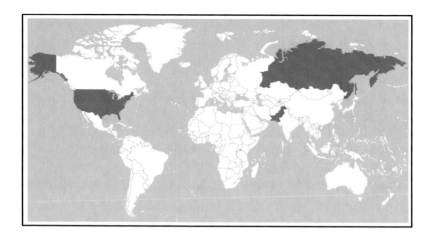

The nuclear-weapon states do not intend to abolish their nuclear weapons. They promised to do so when they signed the Nuclear Non-Proliferation Treaty (NPT) of 1970.

Furthermore, the International Court in The Hague concluded in its advisory opinion more than 20 years ago that these states were obliged to negotiate and bring to a conclusion such negotiations on complete nuclear disarmament.

The nuclear-weapon states disregard this obligation. On the contrary, they invest enormous sums in the modernization of these weapons of global destruction.

It is difficult today to raise a strong opinion in the nuclear-weapon states for nuclear disarmament. One reason is that the public sees the risk of a nuclear war between these states as so unlikely that it can be disregarded.

It is then important to remind ourselves that we were for decades, during the Cold War, threatened by extinction by nuclear war. We were not aware at that time how close we were.

In this article I will summarize some of the best-known critical situations. Recently published evidence shows that the danger was considerably greater than we knew at the time.

The risk today of a nuclear omnicide—killing all or almost all humans—is probably smaller than during the Cold War, but the risk is even today real and it may be rising. That is the reason

I wish us to remind ourselves again: as long as nuclear weapons exist we are in danger of extermination.

Nuclear weapons must be abolished before they abolish us.

Stanislav Petrov: The Man Who Saved the World

1983 was probably the most dangerous year for mankind ever in history. We were twice close to a nuclear war between the Soviet Union and the USA. But we did not know that.

The situation between the USA and the Soviet Union was very dangerous. In his notorious speech in March 1983, President Reagan spoke of the "Axis of Evil" states in a way that seriously upset the Soviet leaders. The speech ended the period of mutual cooperation, which had prevailed since the Cuba Missile Crisis.

In the Soviet Union many political and military leaders were convinced that the USA would launch a nuclear attack.

Peter Handberg, a Swedish journalist, has reported of meetings with men who at that time watched over sites where the intercontinental missiles were stored. These men strongly believed that an American attack was imminent and they expected a launch order.

In Moscow, the leaders of the Communist party prepared for a counter attack. The head of the KGB, the foreign intelligence agency, General Ileg Kalunin, had ordered his agents in the world to watch for any sign of a large attack on the Mother Country.

A previous head of the KGB, Jurij Andropov, was now leader of the country. He was severely ill and was treated with chronic dialysis. He was the man ultimately responsible for giving the order to fire the nuclear missiles.

The nuclear arms race was intense. The USA and the Soviet Union were both arming the "European Theater" with medium-distance nuclear missiles. President Reagan's "Star Wars" program was a source of much anxiety on the Russian side. The belief was that the USA was trying to obtain a first strike capacity.

In Russia, a Doomsday machine was planned—a system that would automatically launch all strategic nuclear weapons if contact with the military and political leaders of the country was completely disabled.

Stanislov Petrov

The increased risk of war was felt particularly strongly by those in Russia who were ordered to prepare for an immediate response in case of a nuclear attack. The command center situated in the military city Serpukov-15 was the hub for the vigilance, evaluating reports from satellites in space and radar stations at the borders. Colonel Stanislav Petrov was ordered to take the watch on the evening of September 25, instead of a colleague who had called in sick.

Late in the evening, the alarm sounded. A missile had apparently been fired from the American west coast. Soon two were detected; finally four. The computer warned that the probability of an attack was at the highest level.

Petrov should now, according to the instructions, immediately report that an American attack had been discovered.

Against orders, he decided to wait. He knew that if he reported a nuclear attack a global war would be likely. The USA, the Soviet Union, and most of mankind would be exterminated. Petrov waited for more information.

He found it very unlikely that the USA had launched only a few missiles. Petrov was well informed about the computer system and he knew that it was not perfect.

After a long wait the "missiles" disappeared from the screens. The explanation came at last: There was a glitch in the computer system.

Petrov had himself been involved in developing the system. Maybe this special knowledge saved us? Or unusual self-confidence and courage in an unusual individual?

This fateful event became known when a superior officer, who had criticized omissions in Petrov's records of the evening, told the story on his deathbed. Petrov has received rather little recognition in Russia.

What happened that critical night—and Petrov's part in the story—is played out in a recent movie by the Danish producer Peter Anthony: "The man who saved the world."

"Able Archer": A NATO Exercise Which Could Have Become the Last

Just like the "Petrov incident," the "Able Archer" crisis was known only to a few military and political leaders in Russia and the USA until decades later. Only in 2013 could the Nuclear Information Service get access to the classified US file. Important documents from Russia and Great Britain are still not available. Why do our leaders feel they need to "protect" us against the truth of the greatest dangers mankind has faced?

Soviet SS-20 Missile

"Able Archer" was a NATO exercise carried out in the beginning of November 1983. The purpose was so simulate a Soviet invasion stopped by a nuclear attack. About 40,000 soldiers participated and large troop movements took place.

Similar exercises had been carried out in previous years. The development could be monitored by Soviet intelligence through radio eavesdropping. What was new was that the tension between Soviet and the USA was stronger than before.

In the background was the Soviet operation RYAN, an acronym for an attack with nuclear missiles. RYAN had become the strategic plan of the Soviet KGB two years earlier, on how to respond to an expected American nuclear attack. The combination of Soviet paranoia and the rhetoric of President Ronald Reagan did place the world in great danger.

Soviet leaders thought that this exercise could be a parallel to Hitler's Operation Barbarossa, the military maneuver that suddenly was turned into a full-scale attack on the Soviet Union.

The Soviet leaders placed bomb planes on highest alert, with pilots in place in the cockpits. Submarines carrying nuclear missiles were placed in protected positions under the Arctic ice. Missiles of the SS-20 type were readied.

NATO concluded the exercises after a few days, with an order to launch nuclear weapons against the Soviet Union and Eastern Europe. No missiles were fired, however, and the participants went back home.

After the exercise the British Prime Minister Margaret Thatcher learnt from the intelligence service how the NATO command had been ignorant of the serious misunderstanding in Russia of the intention of this exercise. She conferred with President Ronald Reagan. It is likely that this information, together with his viewing of the film "The Day After," caused the conversion of the President which was expressed in his State of the Union message in 1984: "A nuclear war cannot be won and must never be fought."

Reagan continued this process up to the famous meeting in Reykjavik in 1986, when he and President Gorbachev for a brief moment agreed to abolish all nuclear weapons before the end of the century.

An interesting and most worrying rendition of how the exercises were perceived in Russia is given in the documentary movie "1983: Brink of the Apocalypse."

The story is based on documents that became available in 2013 and on interviews with some of those who were active on both sides in the situation. Two spies were important in convincing the leaders of KGB that no attack was underway. One was a Russian spy in NATO headquarters who insisted to the KGB that this was an exercise and not a preparation for an attack. The other, a Russian spy in London, gave the same picture.

We can conclude that a lack of insight in the USA and in NATO into the perceptions in the Soviet Union put the world in mortal danger. Did two spies save the world?

A reflection of the danger associated with this NATO exercise plays out in the recent German TV production "Deutschland."

The Cuba Crisis: More Dangerous Than We Knew

Soviet nuclear weapons were placed in Cuba. Fidel Castro and Russia's generals intended to use them if the USA attacked. A Russian submarine that came under attack carried a nuclear weapon. A nuclear attack on the US was closer than we knew.

The development of this crisis has been described in several American books. "Thirteen Days" by Robert Kennedy is the best known and has also been made into a movie. As the story is so well known I will not repeat it here.

In the reports, we can experience how badly prepared the political and military leadership were for such a situation, and how little these two groups understood each other. The generals saw no alternatives other than doing nothing or destroying Cuba with a full-scale nuclear attack. Robert Kennedy wrote that he even feared a military coup!

The US side had little information about plans and evaluations in Moscow. There was no direct communication between Kennedy and Khrushchev. The final Russian answer to President Kennedy's proposal was sent from the Russian Embassy to Kennedy by a bicycle messenger! (The "Hot line" was only installed after—and because of—the Cuban Missile Crisis).

We know less about what went on in Moscow, but Khrushchev's memoirs give some insights. It seems that the Russian generals were greatly worried about the image and prestige of Russia. "If we give in to the US in this situation how could our allies trust us in the future. How could the Chinese have any respect for us?"

The world knew at the time that the crisis was very dangerous and that a nuclear war was a real possibility. Decades later we know more. Thus, Cuban President Fidel Castro, at a meeting many years later with US Secretary of Defense McNamara, said that if the USA had attacked Cuba, Castro would have demanded that Russian nuclear missiles be launched against the USA.

An American U-2 spy plane was shot down over Cuba during the crisis. Only much later were we informed that another

U-2 plane in the Arctic had entered over Soviet territory, misled by the influence of the Northern Light!

US fighter planes were sent to protect the U-2 plane. These planes were equipped with nuclear weapons for this mission. Why? Was it possible for the lone pilot to launch these weapons?

We have also belatedly learned that four Russian submarines carrying nuclear torpedoes were navigating close to Cuba. The commanders were instructed to use their nuclear weapons if bombs seriously damaged their vessel. At least one of the submarines was hit by charges that were intended as warnings, but the commander did not know this.

The captain believed his submarine was damaged and he wanted to launch his nuclear torpedo. His deputy, Captain Vasilij Alexandrovich Arkhipov, persuaded him to wait for an order from Moscow. No connection was established but the submarine escaped. Arkhipov's role has been highlighted in a movie which, like the film about Petrov, is called "The man who saved the world."

What would have been the consequence had the nuclear torpedo hit the US aircraft carrier that led the US operation?

Quite recently, reports have surfaced from the US base on Okinawa, Japan. During the Cuba crisis the order came to prepare for a nuclear attack against the Soviet Union. There was considerable confusion at the nuclear command at the base. An increase in the alarm level from DefCon-2 to DefCon-1 was expected but never came.

A bizarre event, which could have been found in a novel by John le Carré, was called "Penkovsky's sighs." Oleg Penkovsky was a double agent who had given important information to the CIA—the US Central Intelligence Agency—about the Soviet nuclear weapons in Cuba. He had been instructed to send a coded message—three deep exhalations repeated twice—to his contact were he informed that the Soviets intended to attack.

This sighing message was sent during the Cuba crisis to the CIA. The CIA contact, however, realized that Penkovsky had been captured and tortured and the code had been extricated.

Other Serious Close Calls

In November 1979, a recorded scenario describing a Russian nuclear attack had been entered into the US warning system NORAD. The scenario was perceived as a real full-scale Soviet attack. Nuclear missiles and bombers were readied. After six minutes the mistake became obvious. After this incident new security routines were introduced.

Despite these changed routines, less that one year later the mistake was repeated—this time more persistent and dangerous. Zbigniew Brzezinski, the US national security adviser, was called at three o'clock in the morning by a general on duty. He was informed that 220 Soviet missiles were on their way towards the USA. A moment later a new call came, saying that 2,200 missiles had been launched.

Brzezinski was about to call President Jimmy Carter when the general called for a third time reporting that the alarm had been cancelled.

The mistake was caused by a malfunctioning computer chip. Several similar false alarms have been reported, although they did not reach the national command.

We have no reports from the Soviet Union similar to these computer malfunctions. Maybe the Russians have less trust in their computers, just as Colonel Petrov showed? However, there are many reports on serious accidents in the manufacture and handling of nuclear weapons.

I have received reliable information from senior military officers in the Soviet Union regarding heavy use of alcohol and drugs among the personnel that monitor the warning and control systems, just as in the USA.

The story of the "Norwegian weather rocket" in 1995 is often presented as a particularly dangerous incident. Russians satellites warned of a missile on its way from Norway towards Russia. President Yeltsin was called in the middle of the night; the "nuclear war laptop" was opened; and the president discussed the situation with his staff. The "missile" turned out not to be directed towards Russia.

I see this incident as an indication that when the relations between the nuclear powers are good, then the risk of a misunderstanding is very small. The Russians were not likely to expect an attack at that time.

Indian Soldiers Fire Artillery in Northernmost Part of Kargil Region

Close calls have occurred not only between the two superpowers. India and Pakistan are in a chronic but active conflict regarding Kashmir. At least twice this engagement has threatened to expand into a nuclear war, namely at the Kargil conflict in 1999 and after an attack on the Indian Parliament by Pakistani terrorists in 2001.

Both times, Pakistan readied nuclear weapons for delivery. Pakistan has a doctrine of first use: If Indian military forces transgress over the border to Pakistan, that country intends to use nuclear weapons.

Pakistan does not have a system with a "permissive link," where a code must be transmitted from the highest authority in order to make a launch of nuclear weapons possible. Military commanders in Pakistan have the technical ability to use nuclear weapons without the approval of the political leaders in the country. India, with much stronger conventional forces, uses the permissive link and has declared a "no first use" principle.

The available extensive reports from both these incidents show that the communication between the political and the military leaders was highly inadequate. Misunderstandings on very important matters occurred to an alarming degree. During both conflicts between India and Pakistan, intervention by US leaders was important in preventing escalation and a nuclear war.

We know little about close calls in the other nuclear-weapon states.

The UK prepared its nuclear weapons for use during the Cuba conflict. There were important misunderstandings between military and political leaders during that incident. Today all British nuclear weapons are based on submarines. The missiles can, as a rule, be launched only after a delay of many hours. Mistakes will thus be

The Human Cost of Using Nuclear Weapons

The uranium bomb detonated over Hiroshima on 6 August 1945 had an explosive yield equal to 15,000 tonnes of TNT. It razed and burnt around 70 per cent of all buildings and caused an estimated 140,000 deaths by the end of 1945, along with increased rates of cancer and chronic disease among the survivors. A slightly larger plutonium bomb exploded over Nagasaki three days later levelled 6.7 km² of the city and killed 74,000 people by the end of 1945. Ground temperatures reached 4,000°C and radioactive rain poured down.

In Hiroshima 90 per cent of physicians and nurses were killed or injured; 42 of 45 hospitals were rendered non-functional; and 70 per cent of victims had combined injuries including, in most cases, severe burns. All the dedicated burn beds around the world would be insufficient to care for the survivors of a single nuclear bomb on any city. In Hiroshima and Nagasaki most victims died without any care to ease their suffering. Some of those who entered the cities after the bombings to provide assistance also died from the radiation.

The incidence of leukaemia among survivors increased noticeably five to six years after the bombings, and about a decade later survivors began suffering from thyroid, breast, lung and other cancers at higher than normal rates. For solid cancers, the added risks related to radiation exposure continue to increase throughout the lifespan of survivors even to this day, almost seven decades after the bombings. Women exposed to the bombings while they were pregnant experienced higher rates of miscarriage and deaths among their infants. Children exposed to radiation in their mother's womb were more likely to have intellectual disabilities and impaired growth, as well as increased risk of developing cancer.

"Hiroshima and Nagasaki bombings," International Campaign to Abolish Nuclear Weapons.

much less likely. The *Guardian* carried this report in 2014 with some very serious examples of accidents.

France, on the contrary, claims that it has parts of its nuclear arsenal ready for immediate action, on order from the President. There are no reports of close calls. There is no reason to label the collision between a British and French nuclear-armed submarine in 2009 as a close call.

China has a "no first use" doctrine and probably does not have weapons on hair-trigger alert, which decreases the risk of dangerous mistakes.

Why Was There No Nuclear War?

Eric Schlosser, author of the book "Command and Control," told this story: "An elderly physicist, who had taken part in the development of the nuclear weapons, told me: 'If anyone had said in 1945, after the bombing of Nagasaki, that no other city in the world would be attacked with atomic weapons, no one would have believed him. We expected more nuclear wars.'"

Yes, how come there was no more nuclear war?

In the nuclear-weapon states they say that deterrence was the reason. MAD—"Mutual Assured Destruction"—saved us. Even if I attack first, the other side will have sufficient weapons left to cause "unacceptable" damage to my country. So I won't do it.

Deterrence was important. In addition, the "nuclear winter" concept was documented in the mid-1980s. The global climate consequences of a major nuclear war would be so severe that the "winner" would starve to death. An attack would be suicidal. Maybe this insight contributed to the decrease in nuclear arsenals that started after 1985?

MAD cannot explain why nuclear weapons were not used in wars against countries that did not have them. In the Korean war, General MacArthur wanted to use nuclear weapons against the Chinese forces that came in on the North Korean side but he was stopped by President Truman.

During the Vietnam war many voices in the USA demanded that nukes should be used.

In the two wars against Iraq the US administration threatened to use nuclear weapons if Iraq used chemical weapons. Many Soviet military leaders wanted to use atomic bombs in Afghanistan.

What held them back?

Most important were moral and humanitarian reasons. This was called the "Nuclear Threshold."

If the USA had used nuclear weapons against North Vietnam the results would have been so terrible that the US would have been a pariah country for decades. The domestic opinion in the US would not have accepted the bombing. Furthermore, the radioactive fallout in neighboring countries, some of them allies to the US, would have been unacceptable.

Are moral and humanitarian reasons a sufficient explanation why nukes were never used? I do not know, but find no other.

Civil society organizations have been important in establishing a high nuclear threshold. International Physicians for the Prevention of Nuclear War (IPPNW) has been particularly important in this regard. IPPNW has persistently pointed at the humanitarian consequences of nuclear weapons and warned that a global nuclear war could end human civilization and, maybe, exterminate mankind.

The opinion by the International Court in The Hague, that the use or threat of use of nuclear weapons was generally prohibited, is also important.

The nuclear-weapon states do not intend to use nuclear weapons except as deterrence against attack. Deterrence, however, works only if the enemy believes that, in the end, I am prepared to use nuclear weapons.

Both NATO and Russia have doctrines that nukes can be used even if the other side has not done so. In a conflict of great importance, a side that is much weaker and maybe is in danger of being overrun is likely to threaten to use its atomic weapons. If you threaten to use them you may in the end be forced to follow through on your threat.

The close calls I have described in this article mean that mankind could have been exterminated by mistake. Only decades after the events have we been allowed to learn about these threats. It is likely that equally dangerous close calls have occurred.

So why did these mistakes not lead to a nuclear war, when during the Cold War the tension was so high and the superpowers seemed to have expected a nuclear war to break out?

Let me tell of a close call I have experienced in my personal life. I was driving on a highway, in the middle of the day, when I felt that the urge to fall asleep, which sometimes befalls me, was about to overpower my vigilance. There was no place to stop for a rest. After a minute I fell asleep. The car veered against the partition in the middle of the road and its side was torn up. My wife and I were unharmed.

But if there had been no banister? The traffic on the opposing side of the road was heavy and there were lorries.

The nuclear close calls did not lead to a war. Those who study accidents say that often there must be two and often three mistakes or failures occurring simultaneously.

There have been a sufficient number of dangerous situations between the USA and Russia that could have happened at almost the same time. Shortly before the Able Archer exercise, a Korean passenger plane was shot down by Soviet airplanes.

What If?

But what if Soviet fighters had, by mistake, been attacked and shot down over Europe? What if any of the American airplanes carrying nuclear weapons had mistaken the order in the exercise for a real order to bomb Soviet targets? In the Soviet Union bombers were on high alert, with pilots in the cockpit, waiting for a US attack.

What if the fighters sent to protect the U-2 plane that had strayed into Soviet territory in Siberia during the Cuba crisis had used the nuclear missile they were carrying?

Eric Schlosser tells in his book about a great number of mistakes and accidents in the handling of nuclear weapons in the USA.

Bombs have fallen from airplanes or crashed with the carrier. These accidents would not cause a nuclear war, but a nuclear explosion during a tense international crisis when something else also went wrong, such as the "Petrov Incident" mentioned earlier, could have led to very dangerous mistakes.

Terrorist attacks with nuclear weapons simultaneous with a large cyber attack might start the final war, if the political situation is strained.

Dr. Alan Philips guessed in a study from the year 2003 that the risk of a nuclear war occurring during the Cold War was 40%. Maybe so. Or maybe 20%. Or 75%. But most definitely not zero —not close to zero.

Today the danger of a nuclear war between Russia and the USA is much lower that during the Cold War. However, mistakes can happen.

Dr. Bruce Blair, who has been in the chain of command for nuclear weapons, insists that unauthorized firing of nuclear missiles is possible. The protection is not perfect.

In general, the system for control and for launching is built to function with great redundancy, whatever happens to the lines of command or to the command centers. The controls against launches by mistake, equipment failure, interception by hackers, technical malfunction, or human madness, seem to have a lower priority. At least in the US, but there is no reason to believe the situation in Russia to be more secure.

The tension between Russia and the USA is increasing. Threats of use of nuclear weapons have, unbelievably, been heard.

But we have been lucky so far.

As I said in the beginning of this paper, quoting the Canberra Commission:

> "The proposition that nuclear weapons can be retained in perpetuity and never used—accidentally or by decision— defies credibility. The only complete defence is the elimination of nuclear weapons and assurance that they will never be produced again."

Nuclear War Would Devastate Earth's Climate

Paul N. Edwards

In the following viewpoint, in interview format, Paul N. Edwards argues that a nuclear war would affect Earth's climate dramatically. The iconic mushroom cloud formed by nuclear weapons introduces smoke, soot, and debris into the atmosphere that can block out the sun's rays, cooling Earth. Scientist theorize that if enough bombs were used, this effect could cause a "nuclear winter," forcing Earth into another ice age. Recent advances in scientific testing have supported the possibility of a nuclear winter if a nuclear war were to occur. Edwards is a William J. Perry Fellow in International Security at Stanford's Freeman Spogli Institute for International Studies.

As you read, consider the following questions:

1. How would a small nuclear war affect growing seasons for crops?
2. What is the nuclear winter theory?
3. What effects would a nuclear war have on the climate?

In the nuclear conversation, what are we not talking about that we should be?

We are not talking enough about the climatic effects of nuclear war.

The "nuclear winter" theory of the mid-1980s played a

"How nuclear war would affect Earth's climate," EarthSky.org, http://www.earthsky.org, September 8, 2017. Reprinted by permission.

significant role in the arms reductions of that period. But with the collapse of the Soviet Union and the reduction of US and Russian nuclear arsenals, this aspect of nuclear war has faded from view. That's not good. In the mid-2000s, climate scientists such as Alan Robock (Rutgers) took another look at nuclear winter theory. This time around, they used much-improved and much more detailed climate models than those available 20 years earlier. They also tested the potential effects of smaller nuclear exchanges.

The result: an exchange involving just 50 nuclear weapons—the kind of thing we might see in an India-Pakistan war, for example—could loft 5 billion kilograms of smoke, soot and dust high into the stratosphere. That's enough to cool the entire planet by about 2 degrees Fahrenheit (1.25 degrees Celsius)—about where we were during the Little Ice Age of the 17th century. Growing seasons could be shortened enough to create really significant food shortages. So the climatic effects of even a relatively small nuclear war would be planet-wide.

What about a larger-scale conflict?
A US-Russia war currently seems unlikely, but if it were to occur, hundreds or even thousands of nuclear weapons might be launched. The climatic consequences would be catastrophic: global average temperatures would drop as much as 12 degrees Fahrenheit (7 degrees Celsius) for up to several years—temperatures last seen during the great ice ages. Meanwhile, smoke and dust circulating in the stratosphere would darken the atmosphere enough to inhibit photosynthesis, causing disastrous crop failures, widespread famine and massive ecological disruption.

The effect would be similar to that of the giant meteor believed to be responsible for the extinction of the dinosaurs. This time, we would be the dinosaurs.

Many people are concerned about North Korea's advancing missile capabilities. Is nuclear war likely in your opinion?
At this writing, I think we are closer to a nuclear war than we

have been since the early 1960s. In the North Korea case, both Kim Jong-un and President Trump are bullies inclined to escalate confrontations. President Trump lacks impulse control, and there are precious few checks on his ability to initiate a nuclear strike. We have to hope that our generals, both inside and outside the White House, can rein him in.

North Korea would most certainly "lose" a nuclear war with the United States. But many millions would die, including hundreds of thousands of Americans currently living in South Korea and Japan (probable North Korean targets). Such vast damage would be wrought in Korea, Japan and Pacific island territories (such as Guam) that any "victory" wouldn't deserve the name. Not only would that region be left with horrible suffering amongst the survivors; it would also immediately face famine and rampant disease. Radioactive fallout from such a war would spread around the world, including to the US.

It has been more than 70 years since the last time a nuclear bomb was used in warfare. What would be the effects on the environment and on human health today?
To my knowledge, most of the changes in nuclear weapons technology since the 1950s have focused on making them smaller and lighter, and making delivery systems more accurate, rather than on changing their effects on the environment or on human health. So-called "battlefield" weapons with lower explosive yields are part of some arsenals now—but it's quite unlikely that any exchange between two nuclear powers would stay limited to these smaller, less destructive bombs.

Larger bombs can flatten cities. Many if not most people within the blast radius —which can be up to 10 miles—would die instantly. Those who survived would wish they hadn't, since most would die later of severe burns or awful cancers. Radioactive fallout from these weapons' debris clouds would reach the stratosphere, where it would travel worldwide, potentially contaminating crops and livestock as well as causing radiation sickness and cancer directly. Later, this fallout would cause genetic mutations in plants, animals and human beings, as it has in the vicinity of the Chernobyl nuclear accident.

Nuclear explosions would also cause immense fires. The smoke from burning buildings, oil and gas fields, refineries, chemical factories, and industrial facilities would be highly toxic. Forest fires would engulf large areas. These effects would destroy more property and kill more people.

You have asked whether it is legal to start a nuclear war, given its environmental effects. Tell us about the impacts of such a war on climate change.

So far, nuclear weapons have been treated as a last resort. If leaders are rational, political scientists have always argued, they will never launch first because they know they'll be destroyed, or at least badly damaged, by the retaliatory attack.

The laws of war require belligerent nations to avoid damage and casualties to neutral nations and non-combatants. But medium- and large-scale nuclear conflicts would have severe, and global, climatic effects. Most or all neutral nations and non-combatants would be damaged and would suffer casualties. So a strong argument can be made that any such war would be illegal (a point I owe to discussions with Scott Sagan and Bill Perry).

My hope is that as the much slower catastrophe of global climate change continues to grow, the full scale of the climatic damage that could be done by nuclear war will also become a serious issue for international negotiation.

In the Marshall Islands, Climate Change and Nuclear Weapons Interact in Harmful Ways

World Future Council

In the following viewpoint, the World Future Council uses the example of the Marshall Islands to argue that the interplay between nuclear proliferation and climate change threatens the survival of humanity. Between 1946 and 1958, the United States detonated twenty-three nuclear devices on Bikini Atoll. Residents of Bikini Atoll were initially relocated to Rongerik Atoll, which could not produce enough food, causing many islanders to starve. In the 1970s, residents were allowed to move back to Bikini Atoll, unaware of the dangerously high levels of cancer-causing radiation. The Islands are now threatened by rising sea levels caused by climate change. The World Future Council promotes policy solutions that serve the interest of future generations.

As you read, consider the following questions:

1. How have nuclear weapons development and climate change affected the inhabitants of the Marshall Islands?
2. How can renewable energy projects strengthen relationships between nations?
3. How does the continued existence of nuclear weapons threaten human survival?

"Examining the interplay between climate change and nuclear weapons," by Rob van Riet, The World Future Council, April 19, 2016. Reprinted by permission.

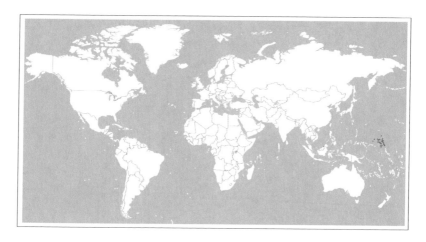

While humanity faces a range of interconnected transnational threats and crises in the 21st Century—including extreme poverty, hunger, pandemic disease and demographic change— climate change and the continued existence of nuclear weapons stand out as the two principal threats to the survival of humanity. On the long arc of human existence, both threats are relatively new to the scene, having only appeared over the last century. Both threaten the survival of life on earth as we know it and both are of our making.

As the Word Future Council has highlighted in a recent report, climate change and nuclear weapons interact with each other in a range of ways. Conflicts induced or exacerbated by climate change could contribute to global insecurity, which, in turn, could enhance the chance of a nuclear weapon being used, could create more fertile breeding grounds for terrorism, including nuclear terrorism, and could feed the ambitions among some states to acquire nuclear arms. Furthermore, as evidenced by a series of incidents in recent years, extreme weather events, environmental degradation and major seismic events can directly impact the safety and security of nuclear installations. Moreover, a nuclear war could lead to a rapid and prolonged drop in average global temperatures and significantly disrupt the global climate for years to come, which would have disastrous implications for agriculture, threatening the food supply for most of the world. Finally, climate change, nuclear weapons and nuclear energy pose threats of intergenerational harm, as evidenced by the transgenerational effects of nuclear testing and nuclear power accidents and the lasting impacts on the climate, environment and public health from carbon emissions.

The Need for Global Action

Negotiations and initiatives for tackling the climate and nuclear threat are reaching a critical stage. At the UN Climate Change Conference in Paris in December 2015 (COP 21), the global community reached an unprecedented agreement on climate change. The Paris Agreement sets out a global action plan to peak greenhouse gas emissions as soon as possible and avoid dangerous climate change by limiting global warming to well below 2°C with the aim to limit the increase to 1.5°C, since this would significantly reduce the risks and impacts of climate change. However, there is some concern about whether this agreement can be enforced effectively. Countries are required to communicate Intended Nationally Determined Contributions (INDCs) to mitigation of and adaptation to climate change which will be regularly reviewed. However, meeting the goals set in the INDCs is not legally required.

Meanwhile, calls from a majority of states for a legally binding instrument or package of measures to achieve the universal prohibition and elimination of nuclear weapons—a goal as old as the nuclear age—have languished. Despite a recent series of interventions setting out the vision of a world free of nuclear weapons by high-level statesmen—including from the nuclear armed-states—concrete action toward its achievement has lagged, although this has the possibility to change with a new process for nuclear disarmament deliberations and negotiations currently taking place at the United Nations in Geneva.

This lack of progress on nuclear disarmament has been starkly contrasted by a renewed focus on the catastrophic consequences of nuclear weapons and recent revelations on the kaleidoscope of risks inherent to nuclear policies and postures. The sobering conclusions are that: a) as long as nuclear weapons exist, their use, whether accidental or intentional, will be a matter of when, not if; b) any use of nuclear weapons in a populated area would have catastrophic consequences on human health, the environment, infrastructure and political stability; and c) the use of just a small percentage of the global nuclear arsenal would create climatic consequences that dwarf the current and projected impact of carbon emissions.

The Availability of Solutions

Overall, the discrepancy between long-term goals and concrete steps undermines the conditions for international cooperation in security and climate policies. Despite growing awareness of the urgency of tackling the climate and nuclear threat among policy-makers, academics and civil society, concrete action is lagging behind.

Why is this so, when considering that renewable energy technologies provide viable alternatives? By harnessing local renewable energy sources, jurisdictions increase their political and energy independency, while the degree of local and international cooperation needed to transition to 100% Renewable Energy can act as a catalyst for cooperation in tackling other transnational security threats. This helps solving geopolitical crises, avoid future armed conflicts triggered by climate instability and resource scarcity, and build cooperative security mechanisms. Similarly, regional initiatives could attempt to tackle both climatic and security threats. For example, Nuclear Weapon-Free Zones (which already cover the entire Southern Hemisphere) can, in turn, promote regional environmental and climate protection policies, as exemplified by the Antarctic Treaty System. Such action could also be sought in the Arctic, where the effects of climate change and the dangers of nuclear weapons come together as increased competition over resources and the opening up of routes for military maneuvering and posturing, including with nuclear weapons, can heighten tensions between the region's powers.

The Legal Imperative

Finally, there exist international legal obligations both with regard to curbing climate change and achieving universal nuclear disarmament. It is thus not surprising that on both fronts, litigation has been pursued to ensure these obligations are implemented. Climate cases have been filed in several countries, including in the Netherlands, where the Court ruled in favor of the plaintiffs, noting that the State has a legal obligation to protect its citizens, ordering the Dutch government to reduce its CO_2 emissions by a minimum of 25% (compared to 1990) by 2020.

On the nuclear front, the Republic of the Marshall Islands filed applications in 2014 in the International Court of Justice against the nine nuclear-armed states (US, UK, France, Russia, China, India, Pakistan, Israel, North Korea), claiming that they are in breach of obligations relating to nuclear disarmament under the NPT and under customary international law. Cases are proceeding in March 2016 against the three of the nuclear-armed states that have accepted the compulsory jurisdiction of the ICJ—the UK, India, and Pakistan.

A Cautionary Tale

For the people of the Marshall Islands, and a rising number of people in other parts of the world, the effects of these two threats are not a theoretical, future issue of concern. Behind the facts and figures are stories of real suffering from climate change and nuclear weapons programmers.

The plight of one group in particular is illustrative of the human impact of the nuclear enterprise and climate change. The inhabitants of the remote Pacific island chain of Bikini Atoll were forced from their homes in the 1940s so that the United States could test its atomic bombs there, bringing with it a legacy of transgenerational effects of radiation exposure, including high cancer rates, birth deformities and environmental poisoning. The lands they had called home were declared uninhabitable. Now, the tiny patches of earth they were relocated to in the Marshall Islands are at risk of suffering the same fate, as rising sea levels are breaching sea walls, washing over their islands, killing crops and forcing the Bikini Atoll refugees to consider relocating again—this time to foreign continents thousands of miles away. As if to underline the potentially catastrophic convergence of both perils, there is even the danger that rising sea levels could spill the radioactive waste from testing, which has been stored on the islands, into the ocean. Their experience should serve as a cautionary tale. If we don't seize the opportunities soon to rid the world of these threats, we will drift toward a similar fate.

Periodical and Internet Sources Bibliography

The following articles have been selected to supplement the diverse views presented in this chapter.

The Economist, "When Nuclear Sheriffs Quarrel," The Economist, Oct 30, 2008, http://www.economist.com/node/12516611.

Lee H. Hamilton, "Nuclear Weapons Are the Most Consequential Threat America Faces," *Huffington Post*, https://www .huffingtonpost.com/lee-h-hamilton/nuclear-weapons-are-the -m_b_11052042.html.

William Harris, Craig Freudenrich, Ph.D. and John Fuller, "How Nuclear Bombs Work," How Stuff Works, https://science .howstuffworks.com/nuclear-bomb8.htm.

Katherine Keating, "Why Nuclear Proliferation Poses an Ever-Increasing Threat," Vice, April, 16, 2016, https://www.vice.com/ en_us/article/jmaw8b/nuclear-safety-facing-the-reality-of-new -threats.

Rose Kivi, "How Does Nuclear Energy Affect the Environment?" Sciencing, April 25, 2017, https://sciencing.com/nuclear-energy -affect-environment-4566966.html.

Robert Longley, "The Art of Atomic Diplomacy," ThoughtCo, September 7, 2017, https://www.thoughtco.com/atomic -diplomacy-4134609.

Lissa Rankin, "Radiation 101: How Does Nuclear Radiation Affect the Body?" *Psychology Today*, March 25, 2011, https://www .psychologytoday.com/blog/owning-pink/201103/radiation-101 -how-does-nuclear-radiation-affect-the-body.

Jacob Weisberg, "What Else Are We Wrong About?" Slate, April 4, 2009, http://www.slate.com/articles/news_and_politics/the_big_ idea/2009/04/what_else_are_we_wrong_about.html.

CHAPTER 4

Strategies for Addressing the Arms Trade

In Colombia, Peace Treaties Ended a Decades-Long Conflict

International Crisis Group

In the following viewpoint, the International Crisis Group argues that implementation of peace treaties is always tenuous. The authors explain how the organization helped broker an end to the conflict between the Colombian government and guerrilla combatants known as the Revolutionary Armed Forces of Colombia (FARC). The violence had begun in 1948 following the assassination of the popular socialist politician Jorge Eliécer Gaitán and the rise of an American-backed, anti-communist oppressive government. It is estimated that nearly 220,000 people died in the conflict between 1958 and 2013, most of them civilians. International Crisis Group is an independent organization that works to prevent wars and shape policies that will build a more peaceful world.

As you read, consider the following questions:

1. Why was amnesty for minor crimes an important part of convincing FARC to lay down their arms?
2. Why was it necessary to address the root causes of the Colombian conflict?
3. Why was popular support necessary for the success of the peace treaty?

"Shaping the Peace Process in Colombia," International Crisis Group, July 7, 2017. Reprinted by permission.

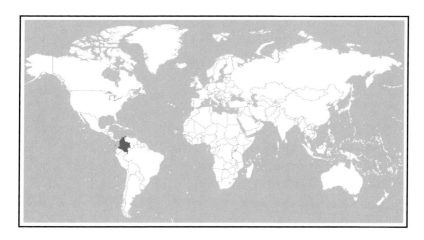

Peace talks started between the Colombian government and the rebel Revolutionary Armed Forces of Colombia (FARC) in 2012, an outcome International Crisis Group had helped work toward for a decade. Our ideas fed directly into the 2016 peace agreement, and helped resolve the difficult tension between securing both justice and peace.

When Crisis Group began work in Colombia in 2002, the conflict between the government and FARC guerrillas was entering its fifth decade. The latest attempt at negotiations had just collapsed, giving way to a tough military approach under President Álvaro Uribe. This policy prioritized security gains at the expense of addressing the conflict's root causes—frequently with disastrous results for civilians caught up in the violence.

We also sounded the alarm for emerging threats. Our 2004 report on the regional dimension of Colombia's counter-insurgency policies was prescient in warning that the conflict could spill over the country´s borders. Four years later this danger materialized, causing a major Andean diplomatic crisis and threats of war between Colombia, Ecuador and Venezuela.

A new impetus for peace came in 2010 with the election of President Juan Manuel Santos, who signaled his ambition to find a negotiated end to the conflict and address its root causes. Crisis Group seized the moment to lay out possible negotiation paths.

A high-level government contact was among Colombian and US officials who praised our early report laying out this new agenda—President Santos's Conflict Resolution Opportunity—saying that Bogotá used a number of our recommendations in initial informal talks with the FARC.

> The analysis of the International Crisis Group on Colombia constitutes an important source of reference that helps us better understand our reality, as well as how to sensitively address key issues such as progress and obstacles on human rights, and the enormous challenges of comprehensive victims' care in our country.
>
> Angelino Garzon, Vice President of Colombia
> February 2011

In September 2012, as formal peace talks opened in Havana, Cuba, our report Colombia: Peace at Last? summarized our private advocacy and quickly became a reference point for media and public debates. In one meeting, a top-level Colombian official brandished his copy of the report, with parts of it underlined: our analysis of post-conflict security risks was of great interest, he said, especially when it pressed for particular care over the reintegration of mid-level FARC commanders.

Arguably the most difficult part of the peace talks still had to be negotiated: accountability for devastating crimes carried out by guerrillas and state operatives in a decades-long conflict that killed some 220,000 people and displaced seven million more. Justice was crucial for a sustainable peace, but the prospect of lengthy prison sentences could easily deter the FARC from agreeing to lay down arms.

> Crisis Group's work is "useful and objective."
> Pablo Catatumbo, FARC negotiator, June 2016.

Crisis Group could combine intimate knowledge of the Colombian conflict with decades of transitional justice expertise: our then President Louise Arbour was previously UN High Commissioner for Human Rights and Chief Prosecutor of war crimes tribunals for the former Yugoslavia and Rwanda, and our Latin America Program Director Javier Ciurlizza had served both civil society and government sides of truth and reconciliation processes in his native Peru and four other countries. We did extensive field work on victims' experiences and expectations, local transitional justice initiatives and the national and international legal context and standards for victims' rights. Our conclusion: a strong emphasis on judicial prosecution for the most serious crimes committed by all parties to the conflict needed to be accompanied by some kind of amnesty for lesser crimes.

Though controversial, we decided to propose a comprehensive model of transitional justice, including an amnesty for political crimes and "effective restriction of liberty" sentences for lower-ranking FARC perpetrators under conditions linked to reconciliation. These elements would be accompanied by an independent truth commission and grassroots initiatives for truth-seeking and truth-telling, and a commitment to comprehensive reparation for victims.

We published these recommendations in Transitional Justice and Colombia's Peace Talks (August 2013), accompanied by intense advocacy with the government and FARC. Louise Arbour met with President Santos, former President Uribe (the principal opponent of the peace talks), and the government's chief negotiator in Havana, Sergio Jaramillo. We discussed our proposed solution across Colombian society, including the victims' groups and activists we had consulted throughout our research. We argued in Washington DC for US support for the peace deal, and engaged key actors in Oslo, The Hague, London and Brussels. President Santos publicly cited our analysis and messages, including in a speech at the UN General Assembly in September 2013. In March 2014, Louise Arbour was consulted by the Colombian government's Advisory Panel on the peace talks.

After many months of contentious debate, Crisis Group's proposals on transitional justice emerged as one of the basic building blocks of the breakthrough agreement on transitional justice that the parties reached on 23 September 2015. Several elements directly mirrored Crisis Group recommendations, above all regarding the distinction between the most serious wartime crimes and lesser crimes liable for amnesty, as well as the selection system for judges in the Special Jurisdiction for Peace. President Santos cited Crisis Group's statement on and analysis of the transitional justice agreement while presenting it to the Colombian public.

> Crisis Group's reports are the "most detailed, realistic and useful" analysis available to delegations at peace talks in Havana. "
> Oscar Naranjo, Colombia's peace negotiator
> and post-conflict minister, September 2013.

The peace deal was signed on 26 September 2016 at an emotional ceremony in the Colombian port of Cartagena as fourteen Latin American presidents looked on. Just days later, however, the process suffered a terrible shock. In a referendum on the final agreement, Colombians rejected it by a margin of 0.5 per cent, and with a turnout of only 37 per cent.

The entire peace process hung in the balance, even if the "no" vote was partly a reflection of the government's general unpopularity. Crisis Group kicked into action, advocating a renegotiation of the agreement with the government and FARC, the opposition and international actors, and identifying ways to mobilize popular support for it. The two sides were already deeply committed to making peace work, leading to a new deal signed in late November and approved by the Colombian congress shortly thereafter.

The UN's Arms Trade Treaty Set International Standards

Rita Emch

In the following viewpoint, Rita Emch argues that difficulties arose when the UN attempted to ratify the Arms Trade Treaty, which regulated the international trade of weapons. On April 2, 2013, the UN General Assembly adopted the treaty. It was signed by 130 nations and entered into force on December 24, 2014. Some nations criticized the treaty, claiming among other things that it violated nations' sovereign rights to arm themselves and favored the rights of countries that export weapons. Emch is a reporter, journalist, and translator for swissinfo.ch.

As you read, consider the following questions:

1. Why did Iran, North Korea, and Syria block the ATT?
2. What would the ATT need to be ratified by the UN?
3. Why was Switzerland considered a "competent and credible" part in the ATT negotiations?

At the conclusion of a ten-day United Nations conference in New York, the Swiss delegation has said it "deeply regrets" the failure to adopt a draft text of the global arms trade treaty (ATT), blocked by Iran, North Korea and Syria.

A first round of negotiations failed last July, after the big arms exporters US, Russia and China had said they wanted more time

"Swiss regret arms trade treaty impasse," by Rita Emch, SWI swissinfo.ch, March 29, 2013. Reprinted by permission.

to consider all aspects of the treaty. In December, the General Assembly of the UN decided to organize a final round of talks, which came to an end on Thursday.

Some 2,000 representatives of governments, international and regional organizations and civil society had gathered in New York since March 18 to hammer out the details of what was seen as the most important initiative ever regarding conventional arms regulation within the UN.

The treaty would—for the first time ever—set international standards for the sale of conventional weapons, tie trade to respect for human rights, the prevention of war crimes and the protection of civilians. Every year more than 500'000 people fall victim to armed conflicts and armed violence.

"Switzerland deeply regrets that we were not able to achieve consensus," Erwin Bollinger, head of the export control and sanctions unit in the State Secretariat for Economic Affairs (Seco), who led the Swiss delegation in New York, told swissinfo.ch.

Dashed Hopes

Hopes were pretty high on Thursday morning that the delegations of the 193 UN member states would adopt the draft ATT text. But Iran, North Korea and Syria blocked the consensus necessary to pass the text, arguing that the draft was unbalanced—in favor of exporter countries to the detriment of importers, among other things.

In the name of a group of countries including the US, Kenya then announced that a letter with a draft resolution would be sent to UN Secretary General Ban Ki-moon, asking him to bring the treaty to the General Assembly for adoption as soon as possible. Switzerland supports this move as well and signed the letter.

The president of the conference, Australian Ambassador Peter Woolcott, will present his report to the General Assembly on April 2.

"Adopting the treaty by consensus would have sent a stronger political signal than a vote in the General Assembly," said Bollinger, who is convinced that the draft text will easily reach a majority.

What Is the United Nations Arms Trade Treaty?

The UN Arms Trade Treaty (ATT) has the ambitious aim of responding to international concern that the $70 billion a year trade in conventional weapons leaves a trail of atrocities in its wake.

The treaty calls for the international sale of weapons to be linked to the human rights records of buyers.

It requires countries to establish regulations for selling conventional weapons.

It calls for potential arms deals to be evaluated in order to determine whether they might enable buyers to carry out genocide, crimes against humanity, or war crimes.

The treaty also seeks to prevent conventional military weapons from falling into the hands of terrorists or organized criminal groups, and to stop deals that would violate UN arms embargos.

Experts say that Washington's signature on the document could be the treaty's watershed moment.

The United States is the world's largest arms dealer. So US support and ratification of the accord is essential to its success.

According to Daryl Kimball, executive director of the Washington-based Arms Control Association, formal support from the United States gives the treaty the potential to change the very nature of the global arms trade.

"The United States already has a very robust set of standards and export controls," he says. "This treaty essentially internationalizes the US system and lays down some prohibitions on the transfer of conventional weapons. And this treaty will require all states to establish export laws, to enforce those export laws, and to abide by a common set of standards."

Conventional weapons covered by the UN Arms Trade Treaty include tanks and other armored combat vehicles, artillery, attack helicopters, naval warships, missiles and missile launchers, and small arms.

The treaty does not regulate the domestic sale or use of weapons in any country. It also recognizes the legitimacy of the arms trade to enable states to provide for their own security.

There is no clear enforcement mechanism in the UN Arms Trade Treaty. It also remains unclear whether the transfer of conventional weapons in ways other than sales—for example, such as rental contracts or gifts—would fall under the treaty.

"Explainer: What Is The United Nations Arms Trade Treaty?" by Richard Solash, Radio Free Europe / Radio Liberty, September 25, 2013.

"Apart from that, the final draft text is much better than what we had last July. Obviously, compromises were made, Switzerland would have liked to see more in certain aspects. But this draft brings efficient regulation of the international arms trade that is supported by the vast majority of the UN member states."

One could say the conference ended in failure, but success was just postponed temporarily, Bollinger said.

Among the improvements Bollinger listed the inclusion of small arms and light weapons in the scope of the weapons covered by the treaty, also that parts and components are mentioned and there are some rules for ammunition and munitions, points Switzerland was intent on having included.

Long-Running Debate

There has never yet been an international treaty regulating the global arms trade. For many years, activists and some governments have been pushing for international regulations to try to keep illicit weapons out of the hands of terrorists, insurgent fighters and organized crime.

The treaty is to set standards for all cross-border transfers of conventional weapons. It would create binding requirements for states to review all trans-national arms deals to ensure weapons will not be used in human rights abuses, terrorism or violations of humanitarian law.

The treaty would not control the domestic use of weapons in any country, but would require all states to establish national regulations to control the transfer of conventional arms, parts and components and to regulate arms brokers.

It would prohibit states that ratify the treaty from transferring conventional weapons if they could promote acts of genocide, crimes against humanity or war crimes or violate arms embargoes.

The draft also requires parties to the treaty to take measures to prevent the diversion of conventional weapons to the illicit market.

From Optimism to Frustration

Ahead of the final meeting optimism had been growing that the treaty would become a reality, but some concerns had remained that Iran or other countries might object.

Iran and North Korea are under UN arms embargos over their nuclear programs, the Syrian government is participating in a conflict that has escalated into civil war.

Amnesty International said in a statement that all three countries "have abysmal human rights records—having even used arms against their own citizens."

After the consensus failed, many delegations expressed their disappointment that just three countries had been able to block this treaty aimed at curbing armed violence and death around the globe.

Non-governmental organizations also expressed their "deep frustration."

"The world has been held hostage by three states," said Anna Macdonald, head of arms control at Oxfam. "We have known all along that the consensus process was deeply flawed, and today we see it is actually dysfunctional."

She said: "Countries like Iran, Syria and North Korea should not be allowed to dictate to the rest of the world how the sale of weapons should be regulated."

Amnesty International called the action by the three countries a "deeply cynical move."

If adopted by the General Assembly, the treaty will need to be signed and ratified by at least 50 states before it can enter into force. It can later be revised, by a three-quarters majority if no consensus can be reached.

Switzerland and the Arms Trade Treaty

Within the UN framework, Switzerland has been active in the process for an arms trade treaty since 2006.

It was a member of a group of experts from 28 countries that handled the preliminary work and later participated in all preparatory rounds of negotiations.

Based on an arms export legislation considered to be among the strictest in the world and due to its humanitarian tradition, Switzerland was able to play a "competent and credible" part in the negotiations.

That it received a seat as one of the vice-presidents in the bureau of the arms trade treaty conference in summer 2012 can be seen as recognition of the Swiss engagement.

During the round of negotiations in March 2013, Switzerland was a member of the conference drafting committee for the final text.

In Iran, a Nuclear Nonproliferation Deal Ended Sanctions

Amanda Taub

In the following viewpoint, Amanda Taub explains the terms of the 2015 nuclear deal that six world powers struck with Iran. The deal ended years of harsh UN sanctions for Iran. Some criticized the deal for not banning other types of weapons as well. While some do not think Iran will honor the deal, monitoring systems are in place. If Iran breaks the deal, the sanctions would return among other consequences. No military response was outlined in the deal because arms treaties do not include military response plans. Taub is a former human rights lawyer who covers foreign policy and human rights for Vox.

As you read, consider the following questions:

1. Why was Iran willing to abstain from developing nuclear weapons?
2. What measures are in place to ensure Iran complies with the deal?
3. What will happen if Iran breaks the deal?

"Here's what will happen if Iran cheats on the nuclear deal," by Amanda Taub, Vox .com, and Vox Media, Inc., July 14, 2015. https://www.vox.com/2015/7/14/8963503/iran-nuclear-deal-violation. Reprinted by permission.

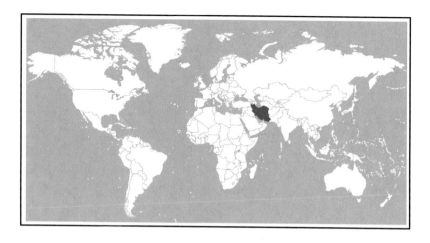

The United States, Iran, and a group of other world powers announced today that they have reached a deal that will prevent Iran from obtaining nuclear weapons. In its most basic terms, the agreement is an exchange: Iran is giving up its capability to develop a bomb, and in return, the US, Europe, and the UN are lifting the sanctions that have crippled Iran's economy.

Iran's government is deeply hostile toward the United States, and there is good reason to suspect that it would at least like the ability to obtain nuclear weapons, so it's natural to be worried about whether such an agreement could really be a good idea. Iran has broken past agreements before. Why should we trust it?

Fortunately, the Iran deal doesn't depend on blind trust that Iran will do the right thing. Rather, it contains strict monitoring and enforcement measures that will swiftly punish Iran for any violation.

So the real question we should be asking isn't "should we trust Iran"—we shouldn't—but, rather, whether the monitoring in the deal is good enough to catch Iran if it cheats, and if the enforcement mechanisms are punishing enough that Iran decides it would just be too risky to try cheating on the deal.

There's a simpler way of asking that question: What happens if Iran cheats? What if it breaks its word and tries to develop a nuclear program?

If Iran Gets Caught Cheating, Sanctions Will Come Back—and Iran's Allies Won't Be Able to Block Them

The nuclear deal actually lays out how all of this is supposed to work if Iran cheats—the negotiators clearly wanted to account for that—and it looks pretty good, if not perfect.

Let's say, for instance, that Iran is secretly siphoning off some of its uranium and centrifuges and shipping them to a hidden site under a mountain somewhere, where it secretly processes the uranium into nuclear fuel that could be used for a bomb.

First what would happen, almost inevitably, is that international inspectors would catch Iran. There are any number of points in the process where Iran could get caught. Inspectors at Iran's uranium mines, its uranium processing mills, or certainly its enrichment facilities would find out if Iran were siphoning off even a little bit of material. Or, for example, they would notice that Iran's centrifuge factories—which they'll monitor—are missing centrifuges.

"The likelihood of getting caught is near 100 percent," Aaron Stein, an arms control expert with the Royal United Services Institute, told my colleague Max Fisher.

What happens next is that the United States, or one of the other countries that signed the Iran deal, can notify the special eight-member commission that supervises the enforcement of the agreement that it believes Iran has "significantly" violated the deal. (The commission includes the deal signatories: the US, UK, France, China, Russia, Iran itself, and the European Union.) That commission has 35 days to try to resolve the problem internally. But if it doesn't resolve it to everyone's satisfaction, then any of the parties to the Iran deal can send the violation to the UN Security Council and begin the "snapback" process that reinstates sanctions.

Once it's at the UN Security Council, there's a very unusual way the violation gets dealt with. To prevent sanctions from returning, the Security Council would have to pass a new resolution declaring that sanctions shouldn't be reinstated. If no resolution passes within 30 days, then the UN sanctions would "snap back" into place. In other words, the five permanent members of the Security Council have to all agree that Iran didn't do anything wrong—if just one thinks Iran broke the deal, sanctions will automatically come back.

This makes it really easy to reimpose sanctions if even just the United States thinks Iran is cheating on the deal. And it means that Russia and China—which have tended to support Iran's interests— wouldn't be able to block the return to sanctions.

Separately, the US and EU would also have the power to snap their own sanctions back into place, basically returning to the status quo before the deal: heavy sanctions that are crushing Iran's economy.

Importantly, under the terms of the deal that whole process could take as little as 65 days—lightning fast by the standards of international diplomacy. That's assuming that the process works, of course, but it's a clever way to ensure that if Iran cheats, international sanctions are likely to come back.

The Deal Puts Strong Monitoring in Place, Which Gives the US Better Military Options if Strikes Become Necessary

Okay, so what if Iran cheats, we catch them, we reimpose sanctions, but Iran keeps developing its nuclear program anyway?

The deal does not spell this out, because arms control agreements by their nature don't get into military enforcement options, but it's pretty clear from President Obama's past statements: If Iran continues cheating and all nonmilitary options have been exhausted, then the US will start to pursue military options. In other words, the US has threatened to bomb Iran to stop its nuclear program, if that is what it takes.

This is another area where the nuclear deal is helpful. As Aaron Stein pointed out to Max, the monitoring will also be very valuable if the deal falls apart, because if military action turns out to be necessary, the information obtained via monitoring will make military strikes much more effective—we'll know just where everything is.

That's really important. Right now, although many hawkish analysts and politicians believe Iran is so untrustworthy that the US should skip the nuclear deal and go straight to military strikes, military action probably wouldn't actually work very well. As Zack Beauchamp explained back in April, to destroy those sites, the US would have to find them. And right now finding them would be a problem, because our intelligence just isn't detailed enough.

But the monitoring from the Iran deal would be much more comprehensive, and so would yield much better information. That means that in the worst-case scenario—if Iran did violate the deal so completely that military action turned out to be necessary to protect US interests—the US would still be better off than if the deal never happened at all, because any eventual military action would be more effective.

However, all of this is of course based on assuming that President Obama would, in fact, choose to bomb Iran if that were his last option. He's threatened as much, but it is an open question—and a source of frequent speculation in Washington—as to whether he really means it. Would he really pick war, especially given that even bombing will not permanently disable Iran's nuclear program? Would the next president?

That's not a question with a known answer, which is why everyone is hoping to avert that scenario entirely. War is a bad choice for the US, after all, but it's a really bad option for Iran, which is much weaker than the US. Iran knows that, and it saw what happened to Iraq and Afghanistan after the US-led invasions there. This is part of why everyone is so eager to avert the military scenarios entirely. But even if the US never actually takes military action against Iran, a stronger military threat will still be a stronger incentive for Iran to comply with the deal.

The Bottom Line: Even If Iran Cheats Taking the Deal Is Still Better for the US than the Status Quo

There's a strong argument that the worst-case scenario isn't Iran violating the deal—it's if the United States walks away from the agreement now.

A big part of the reason Iran agreed to negotiate at all is that international sanctions are really hurting it. And a big part of the reason sanctions are hurting it is that the European Union and United Nations Security Council, which have much more economic leverage with Iran than does the US, have imposed them.

Snapping those sanctions back into place is the US's best threat that it can hold over Iran to scare it into compliance. In order to do that, the US needs to make sure the deal holds together and that it keeps international support. And the best way the US could screw that up is by failing to adhere to the deal itself.

That's exactly what deal opponents in Congress, as well as some Republican presidential candidates, are advocating. They would like for the US to break its agreement with the world powers and Iran and simply walk away; some are demanding that Obama do this, and others are threatening to de facto force it by voting for new sanctions and thus violating the American end of the agreement.

If the US were to really walk away from the deal, then the snapback threat would fall apart. The other countries that signed on to this deal would blame the US for its collapse and almost certainly refuse to impose new sanctions. Iran, meanwhile, would be free from the conditions of the deal—and free from many of the sanctions.

This would essentially be handing Iran something for nothing: sanctions relief in exchange for no new limits on nuclear activity. The US, for the reasons discussed above, would also be less capable of taking military action to halt the Iranian nuclear program, because it would never get the information it needs to make airstrikes well-targeted and effective. And it would not be able to count on European support, as it could in Afghanistan and to a lesser degree Iraq, for its military actions.

None of this makes it impossible for Iran to cheat. It has in the past, and it could again. But if it does, this deal means Iran will be caught quickly and punished severely—it will bear the overwhelming brunt of the pain. Its incentives really could not be clearer.

As New Weapons Are Invented, the ATT Must Be Altered to Regulate Them

Matthew Bolton and Wim Zwijnenburg

In the following viewpoint, Matthew Bolton and Wim Zwijnenburg argue that the Arms Trade Treaty is in need of clear revisions. In order to stay profitable, businesses in the arms industry must constantly produce new types of weapons for their clients to purchase. Advances in technology, like unmanned drones, means that some deadly weapons are not included in the ATT. Some key revisions could ensure that the ATT continues to regulate the sale of new weapons. Bolton is associate professor of political science at Pace University. Zwijnenburg is a humanitarian disarmament project leader for the Dutch peace organization PAX.

As you read, consider the following questions:

1. What kind of weapons are not covered by the ATT?
2. How is the arms industry responding to the ATT?
3. What kinds of changes should be made to the ATT to make it a "living document"?

The preamble of the United Nations Charter states that the purpose of the Organization is to "save succeeding generations

"Futureproofing Is Never Complete: Ensuring the Arms Trade Treaty Keeps Pace with New Weapons Technology," by Matthew Bolton and Wim Zwijnenburg, International Committee for Robot Arms Control, October 19, 2013. Reprinted by permission.

from the scourge of war." The United Nations Arms Trade Treaty, opened for signature this year, contributes to this goal by establishing a potentially transformative new global norm. For the first time, it puts in place international prohibitions on the sale and transfer of conventional weapons to armed groups that abuse human rights and humanitarian law, engage in organized crime or commit acts of terrorism and piracy. The Arms Trade Treaty has the potential to save lives.

But the Arms Trade Treaty will only be as watertight as states' interpretation of it, especially as digital and robotics technology transforms the arms industry. We are in the midst of a far-reaching and potentially destabilizing transformation of the arms industry driven by the growing capabilities of information and communications technology. The most talked-about expression of this is the increasing use of armed Unmanned Aerial Vehicles (UAVs) or drones. However, weapons manufacturers are also developing a wide range of robotic, "unmanned" and autonomous weapons. This includes military land and maritime robots, as well as related parts, components and technologies.

Examples include:

- "Unarmed" versions of the General Atomics Predator XP Drone: General

- Atomics, manufacturer of the well-known armed Predator drone, has exported "unarmed" versions to several states. UAVs are often sold as unarmed civilian aircraft but can be used for military purposes such as target acquisition for artillery or aerial attacks, or observing and scouting of military targets. Moreover, some unarmed UAVs may be armed with modular attachments or through adaptation.

- The iRobot 710 Warrior: This remote-control ground robotic system has the capacity to be fitted with a variety of modular attachments, ranging from a camera, robotic "hand," a shotgun or a grenade launcher. The weapons attachments can be sold separately from the main system and reassembled later.

- The UAS Advanced Development Switchblade: A miniature aerial drone and explosive "loitering munition" (the manufacturers' phrase), launched from a mortar tube, that can be remotely piloted to seek a target and then be flown "kamikaze-style" into a target. Lockheed Martin makes a similar system, called the Fire Shadow.

- Unmanned Surface Vehicle Precision Engagement Module (USV PEM): This remote control unmanned surface vessel can be armed with missiles and a .50 calibre machine gun. It is one of many military marine systems under development by weapons manufacturers. Several navies have also been developing robotic sea mines and torpedoes that would navigate either autonomously or through remote control, detect the presence of a ship or aircraft and even autonomously fire on it.

- The Liberator 3D-printable pistol: Designed by a university student, the plans for this plastic handgun can be downloaded from the internet and manufactured cheaply on a 3D printer.

With an increasing global market for unmanned technology, distinctions between civilian and military applications are easily blurred. Some new robotic systems can be sold separately from the guns that attach to them and thus might not fall into the definition of a weapon (until armed), despite their deadly potential. Future conflicts will likely see increasing use of these weapon systems, providing both states and non-state actors with new capabilities to use lethal force. These capabilities stretch the boundaries of the international laws of war and redefine the interpretations of what constitutes a battlefield. This is already posing new humanitarian, human rights and arms control challenges.

The Problem: The Arms Trade Treaty Relies on an Outdated Categorization of Weapons

Article 2 of the Arms Trade Treaty—the Scope—states that the treaty "shall apply to all conventional arms within the following categories:

(a) Battle tanks;

(b) Armored combat vehicles;

(c) Large-calibre artillery systems;

(d) Combat aircraft;

(e) Attack helicopters;

(f) Warships;

(g) Missiles and missile launchers; and

(h) Small arms and light weapons."

Except for the addition of small arms and light weapons, this list is derived from the categories covered by the UN Register of Conventional Arms, a voluntary international arms trade reporting system. The Register's website clearly states that "Not all arms are covered" by this list, just those "deemed the most lethal."

Later in the Arms Trade Treaty, there are less stringent provisions for states to "establish and maintain a national control system" in order to "regulate the export of ammunition/munitions" (Article 3) and "parts and components" (Article 4). However, there are no provisions for regulating transfers of technologies.

It is clear from reading the Arms Trade Treaty text that its intention is to regulate the broad range of conventional weapons, including the examples of robotic systems listed in the previous section. However, it is incumbent on civil society and concerned states to remain vigilant since some states or manufacturers acting in bad faith may try to claim the presence of loopholes.

For example, the iRobot Warrior falls outside the UN Register's technical specifications of both "Battle tanks" and "Armored combat vehicles." It does not have the "high crosscountry mobility," or the weight nor 75mm gun of a tank. Unlike an armored combat vehicle, it is not "designed and equipped to transport a squad of four or more infantrymen" and may not have a high-calibre weapon. As Unmanned Ground Vehicles (UGVs) become more popular, state will need to consider redefining the UN Register categories to include them.

Arming an unarmed UAV or downloading and 3D printing a gun would, under the current text, be considered a transfer regulated by the Arms Trade Treaty. The US State Department recently acted against servers hosting the Liberator's plans. However, in practical application, there are challenges in the monitoring of these kinds of circumvention, particularly as many new weapons technologies are modular by design.

There is a danger that weapons like the Switchblade (or the Fire Shadow) could fall into a gray area between a "munition" (under the less tightly controlled Article 3 of the treaty) and a "Combat aircraft." It is a fixed-wing aircraft, but given its small size, some manufacturers may try to claim that such miniature UAVs are more like a munition than an airplane.

Finally, the UN Register category of "warship" does not state that it only applies to manned ships. Therefore, unmanned ships and submarines are clearly covered by it. However, it is notable that the USV PEM is not called a "ship" by its manufacturer.

Indeed, there is evidence that some military actors are trying to claim that an unmanned robotic vessel is an "adjunct" to another military ship, not a warship itself. Indeed, if a vessel displaces less 750 metric tonnes, the UN Register does not apply unless it "equipped for launching missiles with a range of at least 25 kilometres or torpedoes with similar range." The .50 calibre machine mounted on such a USV itself would be controlled by the category of small arms and light weapons. But there may be practical problems in controlling those who would attempt to circumvent the Article 4 "Parts and Components" controls by selling such a USV disassembled into modular parts separately from its weapons attachment.

These definitional gray areas pose potential problems in interpreting how the emerging class of robotic weapons will fit into the Arms Trade Treaty categories. Given these complexities, a report from the Stockholm International Peace Research Institute

(SIPRI) worried that the Arms Trade Treaty text lacks some clarity in regulating new weapons technology.

Back in March, while states were still negotiating the draft Arms Trade Treaty, we recommended several key language changes—drawn from proposals already on the floor—that would help "futureproof" the treaty, allowing it to cover emerging technologies. Unfortunately, most of the concerns raised in our paper, as well as by Amnesty International, the International Committee for Robot Arms Control and several states' delegations (including France, Peru and the Holy See), were not addressed in the final text. Amending the treaty (though not impossible) may at this time be both politically infeasible and possibly undesirable while the treaty is being established as a universalized international norm.

The Solution: Ensure the Arms Trade Treaty Is a Living Document

Can the Arms Trade Treaty still be futureproofed? We believe it can, even though the treaty is now final and 113 states have signed it. If used well, the Arms Trade Treaty can become an effective instrument in stemming unchecked proliferation of robotic weapons to criminals, human rights abusers, terrorists, pirates and rogue states. But this will require a recognition that futureproofing is an ongoing task of vigilance that will never completed. Civil society has succeeded in persuading states to negotiate a strong Arms Trade Treaty, but our job now is to win the more complex discursive struggle –that of interpretation and implementation. As expressed by Norway in the UN General Assembly First Committee in October, "The Arms Trade Treaty should, when it enters into force, be a dynamic and living instrument, open for improvements and changes in the future."

The following is a list of options for concerned states, international organizations and civil society to ensure that the Arms Trade Treaty remains a living document, able to adapt to new challenges:

1. Unequivocally Assert that the Arms Trade Treaty Scope Includes both Manned and Unmanned Conventional Arms: The UN Register's definitions, even with the potential problems noted above, include unmanned weapons, because there is no provision stating that they do not. Civil society and concerned states must make this clear in their public statements and call out those who attempt to suggest otherwise.

2. Build on the Recent Definitional Clarifications of the UN Register's Group of Governmental Experts: On July 15, a report written by a UN General Assembly-mandated Group of Governmental Experts and endorsed by Secretary-General Ban Ki-moon, recommended that "Member States report armed unmanned aerial vehicles"—i.e. weaponized drones—to the UN Register of Conventional Arms under that categories of "combat aircraft" and "attack helicopters." The new definitions of these categories now include:

a. "Unmanned fixed-wing or variable-geometry wing aircraft, designed, equipped or modified to engage targets by employing guided missiles, unguided rockets, bombs, guns, cannons or other weapons of destruction," and

b. "Unmanned rotary-wing aircraft, designed, equipped or modified to engage targets by employing guided or unguided anti-armour, air-to-surface, air-to-subsurface, or air-to-air weapons and equipped with an integrated fire control and aiming system for these weapons."

The Group is made up of officials of 15 diverse countries, including the all major arms exporters (the USA, Russia, China, UK, France and Germany). The Group's report represents the authoritative statement on the categories that the Arms Trade Treaty borrows. The Group's definitions should thus be considered binding on the Arms Trade Treaty's states parties. Civil society and concerned states should urge the Group to make similar definitional clarifications of the "Battle tanks," "Armored combat vehicles" and "Warships" categories to spell out explicitly the inclusion of new types of unmanned ground vehicles, surface vessels and submarine/underwater vessels.

3. Develop and Promote Comprehensive National Control Lists: Implementation of the Arms Trade Treaty will largely be decentralized to the national level. Each State Party will be required to draw up National Control Lists (see Article 5, paragraph 2) of the conventional weapons they control, produce and transfer.

Article 5, paragraph 3 says that states are "encouraged to apply the provisions" of the Arms Trade Treaty to "the broadest range of conventional arms." In consulting with diplomats negotiating the treaty, many assured us that their governments would interpret the spirit of the Scope broadly in evaluating transfers (and the behavior of other states). But this means it is up to us in civil society to hold states to that broad interpretation. Civil society, international organizations and concerned states should monitor what weapons States Parties are including on the Lists and call out systems that are missing. "Early adopter" states, the first ones to ratify the treaty, should draw up comprehensive Lists and promote them as best practices, perhaps through regional organizations such as the EU, NATO, ECOWAS, CARICOM, African Union and Organization of American States. Indeed, Article 5, paragraph 4 of the Arms Trade Treaty encourages States Party to "make their control lists publicly available." Civil society could use this to foster a "race to the top" among states—persuading them to make Lists as broad as possible—and shame those which fail to include new technologies.

4. Influence the Interpretation of the Treaty through Careful Monitoring: Ultimately, the strength of the Arms Trade Treaty will derive not from the literal meanings of its text, but from how it is put into practice, which civil society and concerned states have the capacity to shape through monitoring how it is put into practice. This means any monitoring mechanisms should anticipate potential circumvention strategies and hold accountable states, manufacturers and armed groups that try to claim the existence of loopholes.

5. Build Connections to Related Campaigns and Control Regimes: It will never be possible to develop a single, universal control system able to anticipate all the potential threats posed by new weapons to international peace and security. In his most recent report to the UN General Assembly, Special Rapporteur on extrajudicial, summary or arbitrary executions Christof Heyns expressed the need to interpret the interlocking "regimes of international law" relevant to military robotics as constituting "an interconnected and holistic system," each with a "distinctive role…in protecting the right to life." Therefore, the coalition that built the Arms Trade Treaty will need to build links to related efforts like the UN Register, Missile Technology Control Regime, the Wassenaar Arrangement and dual-use equipment control programs. The Control Arms coalition should also collaborate with the Campaign to Stop Killer Robots, the International Committee for Robot Arms Control and those advocating for a convention on cyberweapons to share information, expertise and political support.

Periodical and Internet Sources Bibliography

The following articles have been selected to supplement the diverse views presented in this chapter.

Andrew J. Bacevich, "The Tyranny of Defense Inc.," The Atlantic, Jan/Feb 2011 Issue, https://www.theatlantic.com/magazine/archive/2011/01/the-tyranny-of-defense-inc/308342/.

BBC, "Global Arms Trade Deal Takes Effect," BBC News, Dec 24, 2014 http://www.bbc.com/news/world-30594854.

Anne-Yolande Bilala, "The U.N. Arms Trade Treaty: An Inadequate Solution for Illicit Weapons Trafficking?" Diplomatic Currier, Dec 7, 2012 https://www.diplomaticourier.com/the-u-n-arms-trade-treaty-an-inadequate-solution-for-illicit-weapons-trafficking/.

Frank Jannuzi and Daryl G. Kimball, Time to Curb the Illicit Global Arms Trade, *Christian Science Monitor*, July 9, 2012, https://www.csmonitor.com/Commentary/Opinion/2012/0709/Time-to-curb-the-illicit-global-arms-trade.

Amy Lieberman, "Measuring the Economic Impact of the Arms Trade Treaty," The Street, April 19, 2013, https://www.thestreet.com/story/12792492/1/measuring-economic-impact-arms-trade-treaty-0.html.

Robert Muggah and Nic Marsh, "How New Technology Can Help Us Track Illegal Guns," *Atlantic*, May 31, 2013 https://www.theatlantic.com/international/archive/2013/05/how-new-technology-can-help-us-track-illegal-guns/276440/.

Jonathan Turley, "Big Money Behind War: The Military-Industrial Complex," Al jazeera, Jan 11, 2014, https://www.aljazeera.com/indepth/opinion/2014/01/big-money-behind-war-military-industrial-complex-20141473026736533.html.

Louis Uchitelle, "The US Still Leans on the Military Industrial Complex," *New York Times*, September 22, 2017, https://www.nytimes.com/2017/09/22/business/economy/military-industrial-complex.html.

UN, "Small Arms: No Single Solution," UN, Jan 2009, https://unchronicle.un.org/article/small-arms-no-single-solution.

For Further Discussion

Chapter 1

1. What is the arms trade? Discuss the details of manufacturing, trading, and selling.
2. Who benefits from arms deals? How? Provide specific examples from the viewpoints in Chapter 1.

Chapter 2

1. Why is the illicit small arms trade so dangerous to civilians?
2. Should countries sell arms to nations with a history of human rights abuse? Why or why not?

Chapter 3

1. Why is nuclear proliferation dangerous? Explain in detail.
2. What keeps nations from using nuclear weapons against each other?

Chapter 4

1. How is the arms industry changing?
2. How do international arms treaties need to change in order to continue protecting civilians?

Organizations to Contact

The editors have compiled the following list of organizations concerned with the issues debated in this book. The descriptions are derived from materials provided by the organizations. All have publications or information available for interested readers. The list was compiled on the date of publication of the present volume; the information provided here may change. Be aware that many organizations take several weeks or longer to respond to inquiries, so allow as much time as possible.

Amnesty International
1 Easton Street, London, WC1X 0DW, UK
+44-20-74135500
email: contactus@amnesty.org
website: www.armscontrol.org

Amnesty International is a human rights non-profit. It draws attention to human rights abuses and campaigns for compliance with international laws and standards. It was started in 1961.

Armament Research Services (ARES)
+61 8 6365 4401
email: contact@armamentresearch.com
website: http://armamentresearch.com

ARES is a technical intelligence consultancy that studies how weapons are used in active war zones. They report on how weapons work. ARES is an apolitical, policy-neutral organization.

Arms Control Association
1200 18th Street NW, Suite 1175, Washington, DC 20036
(202) 463-8270
email: tfleming@armscontrol.org
website: www.armscontrol.org

The ACA is a non-profit think tank dedicated to promoting public understanding of and support for effective arms control policies through education and media. They publish the monthly magazine *Arms Control Today*. It includes much of their research into the arms trade.

The Arms Trade Treaty-Baseline Assessment Project (ATT-BAP)
1211 Connecticut Avenue NW, 8th Floor
Washington, DC 20036
(202) 223-5956
email: www.armstrade.info/contact-us/
website: www.armstrade.info

The ATT-BAP program began shortly after the UN began enforcing the ATT. It educates students on what is in the ATT. It also keeps track of which nations are in violation of the ATT.

Beyond Nuclear
6930 Carroll Avenue, #400, Takoma Park, MD 20912
(301) 270-2209
email: info@beyondnuclear.org
website: www.beyondnuclear.org

Beyond Nuclear is a nuclear disarmament organization. They strive to educate and activate the public about the dangers of nuclear weapons. They advocate for sustainable non-nuclear energy.

Conflict Armament Research
email: www.conflictarm.com/contact/
website: www.conflictarm.com

Conflict Armament Research is a European Union–funded project that provides information about transfers of weapons. They track weapons in war zones in order to better understand the illicit weapons trade. They work to lesson the number of weapons ending up in the wrong hands.

Doctors Without Borders
40 Rector Street, 16th Floor, New York, NY 10006
(212) 679-6800
email: office-ldn@london.msf.org
website: www.doctorswithoutborders.org

Doctors Without Borders is a non-profit organization that seeks to bring medical care to those in conflict areas and developing nations. The group was founded in 1968 by a group of French doctors who were determined to bring humanitarian aid to developing nations. Volunteers work to heal some of the damage done by the arms trade.

Federation of American Scientists (FAS)
1112 16th Street NW, Suite 400, Washington, DC 20036
(202) 546-3300
email: fas@fas.org
website: https://fas.org

FAS was created in 1945 by scientists who helped build the nuclear bomb. FAS works to reduce the spread and number of nuclear weapons. They hope to provide science-based solutions for problems surrounding nuclear weapons.

International Refugee Assistance Project
40 Rector Street, 9th Floor, New York, NY 10006
(646) 602-5600
email: info@refugeerights.org
website: www.armscontrol.org

IRAP organizes law students and lawyers to develop and enforce legal and human rights for refugees and displaced persons around the world. It is a project of the Urban Justice Center. It was started by law students.

International Rescue Committee
1730 M Street, NW, Suite 505, Washington, DC 20036
(202) 822-0166
website: www.rescue.org

The IRC is a global humanitarian aid organization. They help refugees with the resettlement process. It was founded by Albert Einstein.

Bibliography of Books

Stuart Casey-Maslen, Andrew Clapham, Gilles Giacca, and Sarah Parker, *The Arms Trade Treaty: A Commentary*. Oxford, England: Oxford University Press, 2016.

Marie Isabelle Chevrier, *Arms Control Policy: A Guide to the Issues*, Santa Barbara, CA: Praeger, 2012.

Thérèse Delpech, *Nuclear Deterrence in the 21st Century: Lessons from the Cold War for a New Era of Strategic Piracy*. Santa Monica, CA, Rand, 2012.

Jennifer L. Erickson, *Dangerous Trade: Arms Exports, Human Rights, and International Reputation*, New York, NY: Columbia University Press, 2015.

Matthew Evangelista, Nina Tannenwald, *Do the Geneva Conventions Matter?* Oxford, UK: Oxford University, 2017.

Martin Gitlin, *The Arms Race and Nuclear Proliferation*. New York, NY: Greenhaven Publishing, 2018.

Richard Haass, *A World in Disarray: American Foreign Policy and the Crisis of the Old Order*. New York, NY: Penguin, 2018.

James H. Lebovic, *Flawed Logic: Strategic Nuclear Arms Control from Truman to Obama*, Baltimore, MD: The Johns Hopkins University Press, 2013.

Dan Marcovitz, *The Arms Trade*. Philadelphia, PA: Mason Crest, 2017.

Tamra Orr, *Iran and Nuclear Weapons*, New York, NY: Rosen Publishing, 2010.

Andrew J. Pierre, *Global Politics of Arms Sales*, Princeton, NJ: Princeton University Press, 2016.

Etel Solingen, *Sanctions, Statecraft, and Nuclear Proliferation*. Cambridge, UK: Cambridge University Press, 2012.

Rachel Stohl and Suzette Grillot, *The International Arms Trade*. Hoboken, NJ: Wiley, 2013.

Lynn R. Sykes, *Silencing the Bomb: One Scientist's Quest to Halt Nuclear Testing*. New York, NY: Columbia University, 2017.

Index